Visions
Of
The Bereaved

Visions
Of
The Bereaved

Hallucination or Reality?

by

Kay Witmer Woods, Ph.D.

Sterling House
PUBLISHER
Pittsburgh, PA

ISBN 1-56315-109-x

Trade Paperback
© Copyright 1998 Kay Witmer Woods, Ph.D.
All rights reserved
First Printing—1998
Library of Congress - 98-85223

Request for information should be addressed to:

Sterling House Publisher
The Sterling Building
440 Friday Road
Department T-101
Pittsburgh, PA 15209

Cover design & Typesetting: Drawing Board Studios

Printed in the United States of America

TO MY BELOVED SON, ANDY.

1975–1991

A SPECIAL THANKS TO MY EDITORS:
SUSAN, CONNIE, SHERRY, AND PRIS.

ANOTHER SPECIAL THANKS TO CHRIS ALAN,
A FRIEND OF ANDY AND TALENTED ARTIST,
WHO DREW THE ORIGINAL PORTRAIT THAT WAS
USED ON THE COVER OF THIS BOOK.

TABLE OF CONTENTS

INTRODUCTION

As a bereavement counselor, I have extensively studied and researched the area of post-death communication; and as a grieving mother I have experienced the phenomenon first hand. The unusual and unexplained events surrounding the death of my only son, Andy, prompted me to research this phenomenon. Because of these experiences, I chose the subject "Paranormal Events Surrounding Bereavement" as the research thesis for my Master's Degree in Transpersonal Psychology.

I have read everything I could get my hands on about this subject, and the more I read and research, the more convinced I am that our deceased loved ones somehow reach out to us from beyond the grave. The message is always the same. They lovingly reassure us they are well and will see us again in the future. When the research is completed and all the evidence is gathered and weighed, I believe we can reasonably conclude there is life after death.

Ironically, I had a strong interest in the afterlife for years before my son's death, and had read most of the books that have been published on the near-death experience. Many times, as I was reading at night, my son would crawl into bed with me, asking questions about what happens to us when we die. I have found solace in the belief that when Andy rose from his body and looked down at the auto accident, he was totally aware of what was happening. I have received comfort in believing that the information I lovingly gave to him assisted him in his own passing.

Because of my strong belief in the afterlife, I felt I would make an excellent bereavement counselor, and was pursuing my degree at the time of Andy's death. This "coincidence" only confirmed how this work is my soul's purpose, and how important it is to let other grieving individuals who have had these experiences know they are neither hallucinating nor going insane. These occurrences are perfectly normal and happen to a large percentage of the bereaved.

My story is told with love to those of you who are grieving. Once you have read all the personal stories, the research, and the opinions of many bereavement experts, you may come to the logical conclusion that post-death communication is not only a possibility, but a reality.

Kay Witmer Woods

CHAPTER ONE

POST-DEATH COMMUNICATION

In our modern society, people are reluctant to speak about what are termed hallucinations. Although recent studies have shown that a large percentage of bereaved individuals encounter some kind of paranormal phenomenon that causes them to believe they have been contacted by their deceased loved one, they are reluctant to relay this information to others. Those who grieve often experience unusual events surrounding the death of a loved one. Maybe you are one of them. Because the population at large has no knowledge of the studies that have been completed and do not realize the frequency of such events, they may be reluctant to share their experiences. If you have experienced such phenomena, you probably feel alone and are afraid of being ridiculed, laughed at, or even thought insane if you tell anyone about them. Even if you have enough courage to tell your conventional psychologist about your experience, you may be informed that your subconscious mind is playing tricks on you in order to fulfill the intense longing you have for the one you have lost.

Historians tell us that long before the dawn of recorded history mankind held a belief in the existence of life after death. No matter how primitive the tribe, or how remote the location, its people held to this belief. Yet in Western scientific circles, this belief is often looked upon as primitive and naive. There is no possible way we could prove the immortality of the soul by using the scientific method. Why must we measure the entire Universe by the scientific rules of a very small speck called planet earth?

In his book *Memories, Dreams and Reflections*, Carl Jung, the famous psychiatrist and theorist, states: "Rationalism and doctrinairism are the disease of our time; they pretend to have all of the answers." Dr. Carol Zaleski, in her book *Otherworld Journeys*, declares that having to have proof of life after death is very characteristic of our "doubtridden and science-bitten culture." While attending a hypnotherapy convention, I had the opportunity to hear Dr. Raymond Moody, the famous author who introduced the near-death experience to America, speak on the subject of life after death. According to Dr. Moody, trying to use the scientific method to prove the existence of the soul after death is "like trying to use the rules of checkers to play chess."

Because of our rational and doubtful society, the bereaved individual who experiences paranormal events following the death of a loved one may question his own sanity, and his fear of ridicule may prevent him from relaying these occurrences to others. I believe if the bereaved realized that many others who grieve share such experiences, they would be more willing to share their own and use them for healing purposes.

Most of the literature on traditional bereavement counseling mentions these experiences. They describe a gentle touch, a voice, a vision (awake or sleeping), smelling a special aroma, an overwhelming feeling of the presence, or a dream visit that far surpasses any dream previously experienced. The dream visit is not confusing or symbolic, but feels like an actual visit with extremely vivid and intense colors and emotions. All of these occurrences, however, are dismissed as hallucinations brought on by the overpowering yearning of our grief. This explanation of these phenomena prevents the bereaved from openly sharing his experiences, for who would willingly talk about having hallucinations?

Ian Stevenson, in an article written in the American Journal of Psychiatry, suggests that because most people who have hallucinations are not mentally ill, there should be a change in terminology. He believes the word hallucination should be used to describe the illusions of the mentally ill, and that the word "idiophany" should be used to describe the experiences of normal people. Because of the stigma of hallucinations being associated with mental illness, many of the people who experience unusual sensory phenomena are reluctant to share them. Stevenson concludes: "It is not clear why, except from the assumptions of Western materialism, these persons should all be immediately judged to be mistaken in their belief."

Stevenson, in an article in the American Journal of Psychic Research, also presents what he believes to be evidence of apparitions which can provide an interpretation of survival after death. He explains how studies about these apparitions have been done since the late 1800's, and if this phenomenon is so widely reported, there must be some basis to it. Although most apparitions are seen by individuals when they are alone, there are many cases where the apparition is seen by two or more individuals at the same time. These collective visions may rule out the theory of hallucination. According to Stevenson, these documented cases happen often enough that they cannot be ignored.

In the book *Regression Therapy*, Barbara Lamb, M.S. speaks of after-death communication,

We become aware of spirit visitations through our various senses. We may see a vivid image of the deceased with our eyes open. Several people may independently see the spirit person in different locations, shortly after the person has died or they may hear the voice of the deceased inside their heads (telepathic hearing) or in the room. They may hear sounds in the immediate environment (tinkling bells, footsteps, knocking, rapping, clicking of a telephone, a child's laughter, a baby's cry). They may smell a scent associated with the deceased person (flowers, perfume, tobacco, aftershave lotion, cooking smells, etc.) or kinesthetically become aware of the deceased, feeling unusual body sensation—the "presence" of the deceased (unusual vibrational sensations, changing in warmth and coolness in the immediate environment, or being physically touched).

We can notice physical evidence of the deceased being present or of having recently been present. For example, without any visible cause, things may get moved, even broken, in front of us or when we are not present. We sometimes perceive with a combination of our senses. With some people there is an intuitive knowing that the deceased person is present, visiting in the form of a live bird or animal who carries the distinct sense of the presence of the person.

Lamb continues by explaining that these visits may happen while in different states of consciousness. Many happen while in a relaxed state such as reading or listening to music or while doing mindless activities such as driving or vacuuming. A visit occurs for various reasons . . . to say goodbye, to give a warning or a preview of another upcoming death, to help in our grieving, to give reassurance about the continuation of the soul, to bring an important message, or to complete unfinished business.

After years of research and study, I have come to the logical conclusion that these experiences are not hallucinations, but actual visits from our deceased loved ones, and those bereaved individuals who share their experiences find comfort and healing through them.

My research has shown there are seven common ways our loved ones visit us. Many times these visits occur when you are in the hypnagogic state, or the state in which you are half-awake or half-asleep. It is at that time when you are just about to fall asleep or when you are on the verge of waking. When you are in this altered state of consciousness, you are the most susceptible to any communication. The following are the seven forms of post-death communication.

1.   THE FEELING OF THE PRESENCE

This is a sudden feeling that you are not alone. You know there is someone near you, and the feeling is overwhelming. It may also be accompanied by a wonderful feeling of peace and love. Although you cannot see him, you know your loved one has come to visit. This experience is so real and alarming, many people state the hairs on the back of their neck stand up.

2.   THE WAKING VISION

These visions appear spontaneously any time during the day or night. You may walk into the kitchen and see the deceased sitting at the table, or you may awaken during the night and see him standing at the foot of the bed. He usually has an expression of love and happiness, and if he communicates at all, it will be telepathically with a message that states: "I love you. Don't worry, everything is O.K. We will be together again."

3.   HEARING A VOICE

You may hear the deceased call your name. The voice may come from without or within. The message will always be one of love and assurance that all is well. This is most likely to happen in the hypnagogic state.

4.   FEELING A TOUCH

This is a gentle touch or a caress. I know a mother who felt a kiss in the morning when she was awaking from a dream of her deceased son. Many times it is a loving touch on the shoulder.

5.   SMELLING AN ODOR

The bereaved smells a particular odor which he associates with the deceased. This could be perfume, tobacco, a favorite flower, etc. The odor is usually overwhelming and fills the entire room.

6.   DREAMS

These dreams are not confusing or full of symbolism as are regular dreams. During the dream, you are fully aware that you are dreaming and in the presence of the spirit of your deceased loved one. This is not a dream that he is alive again, which is a very common dream of those who grieve, but a real and vivid dream which brings a feeling of peace and love. I have experienced several beautiful dream visits from my son, Andy, and I find these dreams hard to express in "worldly"terms.

7. *THE PHYSICAL PHENOMENON*

Objects may move. Pictures may fall off the wall. Radios and televisions will turn on by themselves. I know of one mother whose deceased child's music box keeps going on by itself.

Birds and butterflies are often involved with physical experiences. Elisabeth Kubler-Ross, a world-famous expert in the field of death and dying, uses the symbol of a butterfly on the newsletters sent from her center in Virginia. As a psychiatrist who worked with dying children, Kubler-Ross often had them draw a picture for her as a form of art therapy. She discovered that regardless of whether the children did or did not know of their impending death, many drew a cocoon and a butterfly. Allied troops found drawings of butterflies all over the walls of the children's dormitories in Nazi concentration camps. Many bereaved individuals have some special story to tell involving a bird or butterfly. Through my research, I have come to conclude that, in some way, birds and butterflies are a symbolic representation of the soul. I have included several stories about butterflies in this book.

Time and time again, as I was collecting stories about the visions of the bereaved, people would tell me about how someone in the family, or even the deceased himself, would have a premonition of the upcoming death. Premonitions of death are never included in the traditional bereavement literature, because these experiences are too "paranormal" for anyone with any credentials to go "out on a limb" to publish.

I did manage, however, to find one brave writer. In an article published in *Maddvocate* (the magazine for Mother's Against Drunk Drivers), Janice Harris Lord reports on mystical experiences surrounding automobile accidents as reported by members of MADD. Premonitions before the accident seem to be a common occurrence. These premonitions come in many forms, from a dreaded feeling that something awful is going to happen to a vivid precognitive dream. Lord shares several poems written by teens in which they speak of their own death weeks before their fatal accidents. These premonitions may occur to the victim or to his friends and family. Lord reveals experiences of mothers awaking from a sound sleep with a sudden chill and a feeling of doom at the exact moment of their child's death. Lord concludes by explaining how many cultures openly accept these experiences, and that she feels professionals can do harm to the bereaved when they label them as hallucinations. I agree with Lord.

My own son, Andy, wrote two beautiful poems about his own death about a week before he was killed in an accident. These poems are included in Chapter Three, where I tell of my own experiences of post-death communication.

Maggie Callanan and Patricia Kelly are two hospice nurses who worked with the dying for many years. After hundreds of experiences with dying patients, these two nurses came to realize many of the dying experience precognitive death-bed visions. They label this phenomenon "near-death awareness," and present it in a fascinating book entitled *Final Gifts*.

In the final days and hours before death, a patient may make statements which lead us to believe he is either disoriented or having hallucinations. To make matters worse, many doctors try to deal with the confusion by giving the patient additional medication, and the family may become frustrated and annoyed. These responses make the dying patient feel isolated and alone at a time when what he needs is an understanding listener. The authors suggest if we listen carefully to the dying with understanding, love, and an open mind, they can give us a view of what dying is really like.

According to Callanan and Kelly, the dying often tell us of visions of a beautiful place . . . a place so beautiful and peaceful it leaves them with a sense of awe and wonder. They do not find these visions frightful, but pleasant and reassuring. The dying also sense the presence of, and talk with, departed friends and family members. Many times they can also predict not only the day, but the hour of their own death. They may see religious figures or a bright light. No matter what the vision, it brings a feeling of love, warmth, peace, and happiness. These death-bed visions are not a new phenomenon, but have been reported for centuries. No matter what the time or culture, these experiences have sharp similarities. They tell us,

Such messages have a universal familiarity. For centuries, many cultures have documented aspects of dying, taking notes of altered states of consciousness, mystical interludes, and deathbed visions. Literature contains many descriptions of dying people seeing visions usually interpreted as signs of impending death. Researchers have found sharp similarities among deathbed visions in radically differing cultures and societies.

The death-bed visions of beauty in a place where our deceased loved ones wait for us parallel the revelations given to us by those who have had a near-death experience. And if we choose to believe them, we can find a feeling of peace about our departed loved ones.

Kelly and Callanan wrote the book to offer information and suggestions to not only assist the dying, but learn from them as well. As a patient gets closer to death, he seems to gradually develop this special "awareness" as if he were drifting back and forth from this world to the next. If you allow them, the dying can give you a "Final Gift" of wisdom, faith, and love.

Dr. Karlis Osis conducted studies of death-bed visions in the United States and India between 1960 and 1974 by having approximately 1,800 doctors and nurses fill out questionnaires about patients who were conscious when dying. Osis and his colleague, Dr. Erlendur Haraldsson, found the experiences of the dying to be basically the same regardless of race, creed, religion, or locale.

Although most of the dying patients became more peaceful the closer they came to death, the doctors found that it was not due to medications or lack of oxygen. They also experienced death-bed visions of religious figures, deceased friends or relatives, and beautiful scenic landscapes. The doctors state that these visions were not the result of wish fulfillment or previous belief systems.

Dr. Elisabeth Kubler-Ross, famous for her work with death and dying, tells us about the experiences of the thousands of dying patients she has helped. She says,

> Many of them began to hallucinate the presence of loved ones with whom they apparently had some form of communication, but I personally was neither able to see nor hear. I was also quite aware that even the angriest and most difficult patient, very shortly before death, began to relax deeply, to have a sense of serenity around them. And they were pain free, in spite of having a cancer-filled body. Also, the moment after death occurred, their facial features showed an incredible sense of peace, equanimity and serenity which I could not comprehend since it was often a death that occurred in a state of anger, bargaining, or depression.

After many many years of working with the dying, Dr. Kubler-Ross has come to the personal conclusion there is definitely life after death.

In 1907, Dr. William McDougal, a Harvard psychologist, made a study in which he weighed patients before and after death. He found that all patients lost about an ounce at the moment of death, taking into consideration the weight of air in the lungs. This loss had no physiological explanation. What leaves the body at the moment of death which weighs approximately an ounce?

The psychological literature clearly shows that visions of the deceased are a common occurrence for those who grieve. Not only do these experiences happen frequently, but they bring with them a sense of healing in the knowledge that all is well with the deceased. Most of the psychological literature I have read, however, dismiss these visits as hallucinations brought on by the intense longing of the bereaved. I question why we all "hallucinate" in the same way. Why do perfectly sane people hallucinate at all? If these experiences happen so frequently, might there not be another explanation for them?

Dr. Carol Staudacher, in her book *Beyond Grief,* explains how the longing of the bereaved is so deep and unfulfilled, he creates illusion to fill the loneliness of his longing. She states we may feel the deceased touch our hand or shoulder, catch the scent of his favorite cologne, or sense an invisible presence. Although she explains this phenomenon as hallucination, she does mention that some people believe these occurrences to be actual visits from the spirit of the deceased. There are patients who report having these visits at various times throughout their lives. Staudacher feels why these occurrences happen is less important than how they help to ease the pain.

If I were seeing a counselor as a bereaved parent, and was told it didn't really matter why I was having these experiences as long as it made me feel better, I would resent it. When I had these experiences, I knew they were real, not only because of their vividness, but because I have studied this type of phenomenon for many years. What about the griever who has never heard of these experiences? Is he going to think he is going insane and experiencing hallucinations, no matter how much his counselor assures him that his illusions are a common happening? Would any of us feel comfortable with having hallucinations? When it is not understood, this phenomenon can be frightening.

It is imperative the bereavement counselor handle this phenomenon with finesse and care. In my own counseling, I do not hesitate to relay my personal experiences and share my belief that the deceased may visit us from beyond the grave. If my patient does not accept my belief system, it is perfectly acceptable, but knowing I believe his own experience to be real, and not imagined, must in some way confirm the acceptability of it. All of the bereaved individuals who have shared these experiences with me have found joy in hearing of the similar occurrences of others, for it only confirms the reality of their own. What griever does not want to believe his loved one still exits in spirit? What griever does not want to look forward to meeting the deceased again upon his own death? As a grieving mother, relying on this belief makes life bearable for me.

Brian Weiss, M.D., in his book *Many Lives, Many Masters,* states,

> I believe strongly that therapists must have open minds. Just as more scientific work is necessary to document death-and-dy-

ing experiences, so is more experiential work necessary in the field. Therapists need to consider the possibility of life after death and integrate it into their counseling. They do not have to use hypnotic regressions, but they should keep their minds open, share their knowledge with the patients and not discount their patients' experiences.

Another paranormal event mentioned by Staudacher is the dream visit. She explains how these dreams are very vivid and how important conversations and deep feelings may be exchanged during these dreams. Such an experience can give the bereaved a sense he is being watched over. Staudacher labels these dream experiences "subconscious coping," and believes they are not only a subconscious way of relieving anxiety, but are also a way of fulfilling our wishes.

I have had several dream visits from my son, Andy, and I know the difference between a symbolic dream and a dream visit. Any griever who has experienced a dream visit must have some inkling that this was not just another dream. This knowing cannot be explained in scientific terms. Can we define or scientifically prove the existence of love? But do we know that it exists? My inner knowing affirms the reality of my dream visits. They are not "subconscious coping," and I would resent anyone who told me so.

The famous psychologist, Carl Jung, mentions such a dream visit in his book, *Memories, Dreams, and Reflections.* He speaks of seeing his deceased wife in a dream that was "more like a vision," and explains how his dreams and the dreams of others helped him to revise his views about life after death.

In his book *Grief Therapy and Grief Counseling*, Dr. William Worden presents similar phenomena. He reports how the sense of the presence happens when the griever feels the deceased is in the same area of time and space, and attributes this feeling to a fulfillment of the yearning for the lost loved one. Worden also describes visual and auditory hallucinations as frequent experiences of the bereaved. When speaking of these hallucinations, he states, "With all of the recent interest in mysticism and spirituality, it is interesting to speculate on whether these are really hallucinations or possibly some other kind of metaphysical phenomenon." I appreciate Dr. Worden's willingness to accept the possibility that these phenomena may not be hallucinations.

The experiences mentioned in Catherine Sander's book, *Grief, the Mourning After*, parallel those of her peers. She mentions sensing the presence and also describes an experience she calls the "flicker phenomenon," which she defines as: "A perception in the peripheral vision of the eye seen as a flickering shadow. Immediately, thoughts of the deceased come to mind, but when the bereaved quickly turns to look, nothing is there."

Once, when in a conversation with a well-known psychic, she explained to me how, when we initially begin to see "beyond the veil" into other realms of existence, it will occur as a flash seen from the corner of the eye. She mentioned, as did Sanders, that when you turn to look, it will be gone. She assured me, however, with practice and determination, one can eventually be able to use intuition and personal psychic powers to see what has just "flickered" by. I have had several bereaved individuals describe the exact same experience to me.

Elsie Sechrist, in her book, *Death Does Not Part Us*, gives an example of the "flicker phenomenon." This amazing story is only one of many that Sechrist collected and presented in her fascinating book:

> I awoke at two o'clock in the morning, lying on my back in a state of total paralysis. I could not even move my eyes to the right or the left, but could see only peripherally. I became terrified, but I was unable to call out to my roommates for help.
>
> I then noticed, within my peripheral range of vision, a small object floating by the upper left corner of the facing wall. It was a yellow butterfly, with the markings of a monarch; but in the center was the image of a human face. The face resembled by friend T.P., but I did not sense that it was he. At this point my fear was becoming unbearable, bordering on complete panic.
>
> The butterfly then floated toward me from the upper left, touched me upon the heart, and drifted away to the upper right until it disappeared. At the moment it touched my heart, all my fears and tension melted away. I calmly rolled over, noted the time on my alarm clock, and fell back to sleep until late in the morning.
>
> I learned later that T.P. had been killed in an automobile accident just prior to my experience. Interestingly, he had once had a premonition of his early demise. This forewarning had led to his being tested at the state university, but no ESP abilities were detected.
>
> Even now, writing of this experience has a very strong emotional impact on me. In my mind I have come to understand the butterfly as my deceased friend, in distress at his own passing, returning to console me. Several months after the incident, I came across the information that the butterfly motif had been used by ancient Egyptians as a representation of the resurrected soul.

Candy Lightner, author of *Giving Sorrow Words*, suggests we be open to the paranormal experience. She explains how these experiences can come in the form of seeing, hearing, or sensing the presence of the deceased. Lightner believes most people are silent about these experiences because many individuals, including professionals, discount such occurrences as products of wishful thinking. She presents a quote from Louis LaGrand, Ph.D., professor at the State University of New York in Potsdam: "My guess is that probably forty to fifty percent of the people who have close, intense relationships with somebody who died have some sort of paranormal experience."

Lightner says she realizes that just because these experiences are common, they prove nothing scientifically. They can, however, console the bereaved with a sense that all is well with their loved one. Lightner, after the death of her daughter, founded the organization MADD (Mothers Against Drunk Drivers). Their national newsletter, MADDVOCATE, shares the paranormal events of their readers in a column labeled "Mystical Experiences."

During my research, there was one "hallucination" aspect of particular interest to me. I could not find any instances of people hallucinating about loved ones who were lost to them for reasons other than death. Losing someone you love is extremely painful, no matter how you lose them. Parents may become estranged from their children. The one we love leaves us for another. These are devastating life-changing loses. I have never read of a parent of a runaway having an hallucination that his child has come to say that all is well. An unwanted divorce is a loss in which we go through the traditional stages of grief. Why doesn't a woman who is yearning for her missing husband hallucinate that he has returned? Why doesn't he visit her in a dream and assure her that all will be well? Why doesn't the psychological term "subconscious coping" apply here? I have never found literature that states (as does the literature about the bereaved) that 40 to 60 percent of those who lose a spouse through divorce had a dream visit or waking vision of him.

Why are these visits only from people who have died? My answer, of course, is that the dead are able to communicate in ways the living are not. Those who have died return to us offering the assurance that all will be well and we will eventually be reunited. They alone are able to manifest, give a message, and then disappear.

The parapsychological scientific community has proven there are aspects to the human mind which cannot be contributed to the gray matter of the brain. Scott Rogo, in his book *What Survives*, claims we cannot ignore the findings of the parapsychological community and its thousands of observations and experiments which have been conducted over the past sixty years. The parapsychological studies have conclusively established that "there are aspects of human consciousness that simply cannot be reasonably reduced to materialistic explanation." Therefore, the concept that mind equals brain is incomplete.

According to such research, there are four basic psychic abilities:

1. *TELEPATHY* - the transmission of information from one mind to another without the use of any physical means.

2. *CLAIRVOYANCE* - obtaining information through other than sensory or physical means.

3. *PRECOGNITION* - the ability to predict the future.

4. *PSYCHOKINESIS* - the ability of the mind to control matter.

Rogo believes that we cannot ignore the wealth of information which points to the survival of bodily death.
He states:

> The sheer volume of physical evidence for survival after death is so immense that to ignore it is like standing at the foot of Mount Everest and insisting that you cannot see a mountain. This evidence is of many different types—accounts of near-death experiences, out-of-body experiences, and so on—but the most impressive is certainly the evidence of those who believe they have received incontrovertible proof that they have been in contact with a dead friend or relative. This is the type of evidence that we are tempted to dismiss as wishful thinking when we hear about it at second hand. A skeptic can usually find some loophole in the most well-authenticated accounts. Yet when we read perhaps a hundred accounts, all of which seem to point to the same conclusion, it becomes very hard to feel so certain that they all amount to self-deception or willful mendacity.

As a parent who has experienced various paranormal phenomena, I felt a sense of relief when I learned that many others who grieve experience the same thing. While doing research for my thesis, I spent many hours in the library searching for and reading the many psychological studies. I am including a few so that you can also understand how frequently these experiences occur.

Although most of us are not aware of it, studies on the communication with the dead have been done since the 1800's. The first was completed by a group of Spiritualists who organized the Society for Psychical

Research in the 1880's. They published a two-volume book entitled *Phantasms of the Living* in 1816. These volumes are full of experiences with apparitions.

Lindeman, in a study completed in 1944, describes instances where the bereaved experienced both auditory and visual images of the deceased. In his 1970 study, Parks reports that 19 of the 22 widows interviewed reported visual images of their husbands. A study completed in Tokyo by Yamamoto and his associates revealed that 90 percent of the widows interviewed reported feeling the presence of their deceased spouse. Because of the acceptance of this idea in their religious belief system, the Japanese widows were not reluctant to speak of the experience, nor were they worried about it.

In 1973, Kalish and Reynolds completed a study in which they reviewed the paranormal experiences of 434 people. The results of the study showed that, overall, 44 percent of the individuals claimed to have an experience with, or felt the presence of, someone who had died. The greatest majority of these experiences happened in a dream, but others were experienced while awake. In some of the visions, the deceased both appeared and spoke, and in others there was a physical touch or a feeling of the presence.

In 1981, the bereavement team at St. Mary's Hospice in Tucson, Arizona conducted a study of bereavement clients. Along with many other questions relating to their grief, the participants were asked if they had ever felt the presence of the deceased. Fifty-three percent of the subjects said they had felt the presence of their loved one. The experiences reported were auditory, visual, the feeling of the presence, smelling a special aroma, and feeling a touch. Most of the experiences occurred when the person was awake, but some occurred during sleep.

The bereavement team stresses the importance of listening to these experiences with warmth and acceptance. It is important to the bereaved to share his feelings about such happenings, for in the sharing he feels a sense of relief. The team did stress, however, that it would be detrimental to pressure anyone to speak of an experience they wish to keep to themselves. The authors conclude these experiences to be of profound importance to the bereaved because they help him to know his loved one is safe and happy, and that he can now go on with his life.

From 1980 to 1981, the Gallup Organization conducted a series of national surveys into American beliefs about immortality. In the book, *Adventures in Immortality*, George Gallup, Jr. presents an examination of the results of this survey. According to the survey, not only have eight million Americans had a near-death experience, but many people believe they have caught a glimpse of eternity through dreams, spiritual visions, and other unusual occurrences.

Gallup states that one out of every ten adults (15 million people) believe that the dead can minister to the needs of the people on earth. Many of these people believe that through dreams and visions we can communicate with dead friends and relatives. They theorize the dead may have a bigger perspective on life and may be able to help the living with the important decisions they need to make. Those who experience near-death tell us that our deceased loved ones are there to greet us when we die. When asked if it is possible to communicate with the dead, about 24 percent of the population (37 Million) stated yes, they believe it is possible.

Other results of this extensive survey show that not only do two-thirds of the American public (about 100 million people) believe that there is life after death, but one third of all Americans (47 million) have had some kind of mystical experience. These experiences may include a feeling of complete union with the universe, communication with deceased loved ones, visions of unusual lights, and out-of-body experiences. The mystical experiences seem to have many common elements with near-death.

In an enlightening article in American Health Magazine, Andrew Greeley reports new data on communications with the dead. His study, completed at the University of Chicago's National Opinion Research Council in 1984, was the second of two such studies. This second study shows that the percentage of Americans who are reporting extra-sensory experiences is on the rise. Greeley states: "Such paranormal experiences are generally viewed as hallucinations or symptoms of mental disorder. But if these experiences were signs of mental illness, our numbers would show the country is going nuts! What was paranormal is now normal."

An interesting point which the study revealed was how many of the widows who had these experiences had not previously believed in an afterlife. Greeley feels this shows they were not envisioning an experience that would confirm their belief system. He believes these findings make it difficult to explain such occurrences as just "psychological wish fulfillment;" and concludes that these experiences are happening on such a large scale, they could "change the nature of our society."

One of the most recent articles presented on the subject of post-death communication was published in the winter of 1992 edition of *Near-Death Studies*. In this article, Raymond Moody tells of visionary encounters with the departed in his modern-day psychomanteum. Moody begins by reporting that apparitions of the deceased by the bereaved are extremely common, and those who experience these encounters are totally convinced of the reality of the experience.

While completing his research, Moody found that the ancient Greeks used psychomanteums, or oracles of the dead, where people journeyed for consultations with the spirits of the departed. In these oracles, seekers gazed into clear water in order to see the deceased.

Moody explains how mankind has used crystal balls, clear water, and mirrors since ancient times to receive visions of other realms. The visions were usually colored and three dimensional. The ancients used crystal gazing for fortune telling, locating lost objects, visiting with the dead, and seeing events which were happening a great distance away.

Crystal gazing was not only used by native Americans, but also in the ancient oracles of Tibet and Medieval Europe. The Aztecs used a polished obsidian stone for purposes of divination. Using a reflective surface to contact spirits is mentioned in the works of Homer, Plato, the Bible, and many other archaic texts.

Moody created his own psychomanteum for the purpose of inducing these visions under controlled circumstances. Through the use of lighting, mirrors, music, and relaxation techniques, Moody guided 29 people through the procedure, and 16 experienced apparitions. Not only did these visions appear, but in six of the cases they spoke and held conversations with the experimenter. Some of the apparitions actually emerged from the mirror. These experiences did not seem strange or uncomfortable, but quite natural. The encounter seemed to be a healing one, with the emphasis upon the relationship between the living and the deceased. Moody reports, "Many persons who experience apparitions of deceased loved ones relate that the episodes result in an alleviation or even a resolution of their grief. Subjects, who encountered apparitions in the present study, experienced the events primarily as healings of the relationships with the deceased persons. It is conceivable that in the future, therapeutic techniques might be derived from investigations like this one."

Bonnie Lindstrom is the director of Community Hospice in Tucson, Arizona. The Seattle Times presented an article entitled "Communication with the Deceased" in which Lindstrom declares her belief in this phenomenon. According to her experience, "Communication with the deceased is so common, we don't make note of it anymore; it's just part of every day." She adds, "These are normal experiences to a loss, and it doesn't mean that people are crazy."

Lindstrom estimates that 60 to 70 percent of bereaved individuals experience some kind of post-death communication. Both MADD (Mothers Against Drunk Drivers) and the Compassionate Friends (a national support group of bereaved parents) report numerous accounts of these happenings. Through her experience of working with hospice, she has found most of these occurrences to be positive and to relay messages of love, hope, forgiveness, and encouragement. Lindstrom concludes, "For people who are grieving, it often is a turn around. They may be depressed and then they have an experience like this, and it changes things overnight".

In the book, *Creativity in Death Education and Counseling*, Lindstrom presents a chapter entitled "Exploring Paranormal Experiences of the Bereaved". She relays her belief that such experiences are a natural phenomenon. Throughout the six years she has been counseling bereaved families, she has found that more than half of them recount fascinating stories. Lindstrom lists the paranormal experiences as intuitive, visual, auditory, olfactory, tactile, and dreams. Dreams seem to be the most common type of communication. Many of the dreams are recurring, and seem to show that the deceased needs to conclude some "unfinished business."

Although these experiences may occur at any time of the day, Lindstrom has found they usually do so in the evening. These events are sometimes shared by two or more individuals which helps to rule out the possibility of hallucination. The bereaved do not believe these experiences are hallucinations, but are true profound visits by their deceased loved ones. These visits are both reassuring and encouraging, and not only give the bereaved a sense all is well with the departed, but also give them feelings of comfort, peace, and happiness. The griever now feels the departed is fine, and he can go on with his life. Knowing others have shared these experiences affirms to the bereaved that he is not alone and helps to confirm his belief that his experience is not hallucination.

Lindstrom stresses the importance of the bereavement counselor to accept these experiences with warmth and openness, and concludes by mentioning how the research in this area is limited by the reluctance of many professionals to delve into anything paranormal.

The preceding information is only a small part of the psychological literature on this subject, and there are many more articles and studies available which I have not included. What has been presented, however, should give you a general idea that this phenomenon has been previously explored. Although the visions of the bereaved have been extensively researched and studied, information about them has not been made available to the general public. Therefore, most of the grieving individuals who experience these visits do not realize they share a common ground with many others who grieve. I have found comfort in knowing that I am not alone.

Why does our Western society have to dismiss these occurrences as hallucinations? Are all of the bereaved deranged? . . . suffering from illusions? . . . lying about their experiences? Our science-bitten culture does not want to accept the possibility that our deceased loved ones come to us from beyond the grave, even if their message is one of hope, love, and the continuation of life. According to the last Gallup pole, eight million Americans have had a near-death experience. Are they also hallucinating? It is time for the psychological community to recognize these experiences for the comfort they bring, and discontinue labeling them "hallucinations."

In conclusion, I would like to express that it would be just as unfair for me to assume ALL of these experiences to be visitations as it would be for someone else to dismiss them as hallucinations. When using the scientific method, we are supposed to gather all possible data, and then weigh the evidence. For someone in the psychological community to dismiss the thousands of experiences of the bereaved without careful study is certainly not scientific. The mind is a vast and wondrous thing. Some "visits" may be hallucinations . . . some dreams may be just dreams, but when all the evidence has been gathered, one could make the logical assumption that communication with the deceased is not only a possibility but a reality.

CHAPTER TWO

THE NEAR-DEATH AND OUT-OF-BODY EXPERIENCE

In my opinion, our culture is experiencing a new paradigm, an expanded belief about our spiritual nature. When we live within a certain paradigm we can only see things one way; but when the paradigm shifts, the old way of seeing things changes.

I believe those who dismiss such events as the near-death or the paranormal experience could be thought of as part of the "Old Paradigm." Those who work within the realm of the "New Paradigm" take what is good from the old way of thinking, and then proceed to openly evaluate new ways of thinking and perceiving. The paradigm shift which is happening today is helping us to realize that we, as humans, are not only made up of mind and body, but also of spirit. We must learn to go beyond what is "tried and true" and begin to realize, as we come to the close of this century, we are learning more and more about our inner nature.

In the preface to his book, *Heading Toward Omega*, Kenneth Ring declares that "humanity as a whole is collectively struggling to awaken to a new and higher mode of consciousness." He believes the NDE (near-death experience) can be viewed as an "evolutionary device" to bring about a new transformation of mankind. He says, "My thesis is, in short, that we ourselves are witnesses to a major evolutionary metamorphosis in the human race and that many NDEers—as well as others who have had functionally similar awakenings—are in the leading edge of this evolutionary wave."

The discovery of the NDE has profoundly contributed to the paradigm shift. The first book to come on the American scene was Raymond Moody's *Life After Life* in 1975. In this best-seller, Moody coined the phrase "near-death experience." Since then, there has been a wealth of studies, articles, and books concerning the subject. The idea of the near-death experience has been incorporated into many television shows and has been discussed on numerous talk shows including "Oprah Winfrey." Most Americans are familiar with at least the term.

Dr. Michael Sabom, a cardiologist at Georgia's Emory University School of Medicine, completed a study in 1976 in which he interviewed 100 patients who had experienced clinical death. The results of his study showed that 61 percent of those interviewed had experiences which were similar to those reported by Raymond Moody. Dr. Sabom is particularly impressed by how many patients can accurately describe complex medical techniques which are performed on them during surgery. Dr. Sabom has concluded that the near-death experience cannot be dismissed as an illusion.

Melvin Morse, M.D. completed a study on the near-death experiences of children at the University of Washington, Seattle. He says,

> Children have simple and pure near-death experiences, untroubled by religious or cultural expectations. They do not suppress the experience as adults often do and have no trouble accepting the spiritual implications of seeing God. I will never forget a five year old girl who shyly told me: "I talked to Jesus and he was nice. He told me that it wasn't my time to die." Children remember their near-death experiences far more often than adults do, and as a result of their experience they seem to have an easier time accepting and understanding their own spirituality as adults. If they have another near-death experience as an adult, it is usually exceptionally powerful and complete.

In her book, *Regression Therapy*, Winafred Blake Lucas, Ph.D. states,

> Death appears to those who have approached it in the near-death experience to be a transition, not an ending. The essence of us remains, along with such learning as has been gleaned in lifetime just over. Gradually the concept that we are the victims of death, laid low by the "grim reaper," is becoming seen as invalid and inaccurate. The new conceptualization also outmodes our current cultural behavior that fights desperately to keep those we love from dying. We are moving into a time when we can help each other make our transitions joyously and with awareness, rather than as passive victims.

IANDS (International Association of Near-Death Studies, Inc.) is located in Windsor Hill, Connecticut. According to their brochure, its purpose is "to support exploration of the experience, not to offer any one explanation of it. The Association is committed to the scientifically-grounded investigation of the NDE and to providing accurate information based on those findings."

According to IANDS, no two NDE'S are exactly alike, but there is a pattern to them, and every experience includes one or more of the following:

1. Feeling that the "self" has left the body. Often the "self" moves overhead and "watches" efforts to revive the physical body. The person may later be able to describe who was there and what happened, sometimes in detail.
2. Moving through a dark space or "tunnel."
3. Encountering a radiant light. It is usually described as golden or white, and as being magnetic or loving.
4. Feeling at one with the universe; having a sense of understanding everything, or knowing "how the world works."
5. Meeting others, possibly deceased family and friends.
6. Having a life review, "seeing my life pass in front of me."
7. Reaching a boundary—a cliff, water, some kind of barrier that may not be crossed if one is to return to life.
8. In rare cases, entering a landscape or city.
9. Returning to the body.

According to IANDS, millions of people have had the experience, and about 35% of those people who have come close to death report having an NDE.

Who has such experiences? IANDS tells us, "The NDE occurs to sane and normal people of all races, religions, backgrounds, and ages, including very small children."

How do people feel about having an NDE? The brochure states:

> A person who has had the experience has very mixed feelings. He or she may be very angry at coming back to physical pain and suffering, and at having "lost the Light." There may be fear of insanity because something has happened that seems impossible. Very often people have deep fear of being ridiculed. Not all NDE's are remembered immediately, and bits and pieces of the experience may be remembered over quite a long period of time. In this case, the person may wonder what is happening. On the other hand, most experiencers are no longer afraid of death. They are also typically sure that their lives have a purpose and meaning. An experiencers may feel special, or "chosen."

Many people who have experienced an NDE have a change of personality, IANDS says:

> Just about every person who has an NDE seems to have a changed understanding of what life is all about. This usually goes very deep and is often impossible for the person to explain.

Almost always, the person's values change. Besides losing all fear of death, the person may also have lost interest in financial or career success. "Getting ahead" may seem like an odd game, one that the person chooses not to "play" even if it means giving up friendships.

Becoming more loving is very important to most experiencers, although they may have difficulty explaining what they mean by that. They may become deeply interested in service, in helping others. They may become more outgoing. After an NDE, beliefs often change. Religious observance may or may not increase, but belief in a "spiritual reality" is almost certain. A frequent comment is, "I thought this was so before my experience, but now I KNOW." After the experience some people find they have an increase in psychic abilities. No one knows why this happens, but many experiences report it.

The eight-million people who have had an NDE can give us a relatively good idea of what happens to us when we die. All of the books I have read on the subject seem to agree. The following is an example of a typical scenario of a near-death experience.

I find myself rising from my physical body. I look down and see my own body and the doctor and nurse working on it. At first I observe, saying to myself, "Look at that poor person down there. He's really in bad shape." When I look closer, however, I realize the person is me, and that I have somehow become a detached observer. The fact that my physical body is in such bad shape doesn't seem to concern me. I realize I must be dead, but I'm not afraid. I feel at total peace, with no pain whatsoever. I walk around the hospital, going into the waiting room and watching my loved ones sitting around in grief and despair.

I suddenly find myself in a dark tunnel (it may be a valley, a path through the woods, or a long dark hallway). Far off in the distance, at the end of the tunnel, is a brilliant warm light. I am strongly drawn to it and want to feel its warmth and love. The closer I get to the light, the better I feel. As I approach the light, I begin to see people; loved ones who have died . . . a mother, a grandmother, a childhood friend who died in an accident. They come to me in unconditional love, and greet me joyfully. After I am greeted, I am drawn to a radiant individual. Some call it a guardian angel, some call it Jesus, some call it God, some just call it a Being of light. From this Being, I feel an unconditional love unlike any love I ever experienced on earth. The love is so overwhelming, I never want to leave it.

Next, my entire life flashes before my eyes. Everything I have ever done is revealed to me. I witness all of the unkind things I have ever done to anyone. I not only see them, but I actually feel the feelings of the person I hurt. I also get to witness the ripple effect of my unkind deed. When I am unkind to someone, they turn around and are unkind to someone else, who in turn is unkind to another person. I get to feel the feelings of all this unhappiness. I see and feel all the damage I have done.

Now I watch all of the good deeds I performed, and I feel the warm feelings of the people who were affected by them. I witness the ripple effect of this kindness as it is passed on from person to person. I have quickly reviewed my entire life and see all of my mistakes as well as my good deeds with a mature spiritual understanding. The being of light has been my companion throughout the process and has supported me without judgment.

The being of light (or maybe a deceased relative) tells me that it is "not my time" and I must return, for there is work left for me to do on earth. (On some occasions, the near-deather is given a choice as to whether he wants to stay or go). When I awake, I am back in my body, but the experience will transform me forever.

Everyone who has an NDE does not have a complete experience that includes all of the various stages. Some only experience rising from their body, some people only see deceased relatives, some people remember being in the tunnel and going toward the light, but don't remember the rest. Some near-deathers do not have a life review. Each experience seems to be unique.

Before the onset of studies of the NDE in the 1970's, the experience was dismissed by the medical profession as hallucination. Neuroscience is now trying to search for a neuro-physical explanation for the NDE. When certain areas of the brain are electrically stimulated, patients have vivid memories as if they were actually seeing them. Some believe endorphins in the brain cause feelings of euphoria and celestial visions. Compression of the optic nerve by lack of oxygen may cause a tunnel image. As of yet, however, a direct relationship between the brain and this experience has not been established.

If the experience is caused by lack of oxygen to the brain, how does this explain how the person experiencing the NDE can leave his body and tell you what was happening in various parts of the hospital while he was unconscious. How can endorphins allow you to know what was going on in the waiting room while you were being resuscitated?

After many years of research, we are no nearer finding a "scientific" explanation for the NDE. Are these experiences glimpses of heaven or hallucinations? One aspect which convinces me of the validity of actual visits to other realms of existence is how, no matter who the experiencer (whether he be someone from Japan, India, Africa, or America), the stories are consistently the same. They follow the same patterns, even if the details may differ. The visions seem to be personal, but yet somehow universal. How is it possible for a three-year-old child to describe a full-blown NDE, complete with the being of light? How could endorphins in the brain change millions of people for the good and make them more compassionate, caring, serving of others, and less interested in making money? Logic would only tell us there is something greater than changes in "gray matter" going on here.

Dr. Melvin Morse of the Seattle Children's Hospital states,

> Near-death experiences are not caused by a lack of oxygen to the brain, or drugs, or psychological stresses evoked by the fear of dying. Almost twenty years of scientific research has documented that these experiences are a natural and normal process. We have even documented an area in the brain which allows us to have the experience. That means that near-death experiences are absolutely real and not hallucinations of the mind. "They are as real as any other human capability; they are as real a math, as real as language."

There are several elements in the NDE that are extremely important to one who is worrying about his deceased loved one; and, if he believes these stories, he can find much needed comfort.

Firstly, those people who have experienced death of the physical body can relay to us how our consciousness survives this experience. Our personality does not change, and we don't suddenly become an angel. We are at peace, have no physical pain, and have a body much like the one we had in the physical world. Although we can see and hear those around us who are still in physical bodies, they are not aware of us.

The information we receive from the NDE is in complete agreement with what is related to us through post-death communication. Most messages received state: "I am fine. I am at peace. Don't worry about me. We will be together again." Our loved ones often give us advice or speak to us of the happenings of our current lives. This information correlates with what the near-deather tells us about being out-of-body . . . he can still see and hear what is going on in the lives of the living.

Another aspect of the NDE which confirms what is often stated in after-death communication is the fact that when we enter the light, we are greeted by deceased relatives. Those who have gone on are still very much concerned about us, and continue to be part of our lives.

Many people who experience near-death are told they must return because it is "not their time." This, too, can help those who grieve. One major aspect of grief is how we somehow feel responsible for the death, and fill our minds with an abundance of "if only's": "If only I wouldn't have allowed him to go in the car that night." "If only I would have taken him to another doctor." We somehow feel guilty because we are still alive and they are not. Many bereaved individuals feel guilty about not having done what they could have for the deceased.

If we can believe the near-deather, then each of us has a time to die. It is not anyone's fault. Some of us are here for eight years, some of us for eighty. Through my many years of study, I have come to believe the duration of our life is predetermined in spirit before we enter the physical plane. An understanding of, or belief in, this concept can eliminate unnecessary remorse and guilt. The reluctance to return, which occurs during an NDE, can reassure the bereaved that not only are the deceased happy where they are, but that we will all be reunited in the Light once again.

Another aspect of the near-death experience which helps us better understand our deceased loved one is the profound change which occurs to anyone who has had an NDE. This transformation has been well documented and results in a greater appreciation for life, higher self esteem, a sense of life's purpose, a love of learning, an interest in spirituality, a heightened sense of intuition (some actually become psychic), and a greater compassion for all people and animals. If those who have had an NDE can experience such a transformation by only being on "the other side" for a few minutes, imagine the transformation of the deceased. The basic personality does not change, but the capacity for love, understanding, and seeing "the bigger picture" of life does. That is why when we experience post-death communication, our loved ones appear to be so loving, compassionate, understanding, and forgiving.

The famous psychotherapist, Carl Jung, who had an NDE in the 1940's during a heart attack, states:

> It seemed to me I was high up in space. Far below I saw the globe of earth bathed in a glorious blue light. Ahead of me I saw a shining temple and was drawn towards it. As I approached, a strange thing happened. I had the certainty I was about to enter an illuminated room and meet there all those people to whom I was beloved in reality. There I would understand at last the meaning of my life.

He also says,

> What happens after death is so unspeakably glorious that our imaginations and our feelings do not suffice to form even an approximate conception of it. . . . Sooner or later, the dead all become what we also are. But in reality, we know little or

> nothing about that mode of being. And what shall we know of
> this earth after death? The dissolution of our time-bound form
> in eternity brings no loss of meaning. Rather, does the little
> finger know itself a member of the hand.

Jung made a study of the myths and sacred writings through history and found many similar images and stories appeared again and again. He hypothesized that mankind must share some kind of internal mental memories of all previous experiences throughout the ages. He labeled this great subconscious pool of knowledge the "Collective Unconscious," and the major recurring patterns of images and themes he call the "Archetypes" of the Collective Unconscious. Could the fact that we all use the same basic archetypes be an explanation for the similarity of all near-death experiences?

Edgar Cayce's theories of the functioning of the subconscious mind parallel those of Jung. Cayce (1877-1945) is America's most well-know psychic. While in a trance state, Cayce could accurately diagnose the illness of an individual no matter where in the world he was located, merely by being told the person's name and address. Along with the diagnosis, he would recommend specific treatments. In cases verified by patients, Cayce was completely accurate in both diagnosis and treatment in 85 percent of the cases. Although many of his treatments were unorthodox, their effectiveness and accuracy made Cayce famous throughout the country.

Cayce's "readings," however, were not limited to health issues. He also gave information on life issues, missing persons, and universal truths. Of all the more than 10,000 readings given by Cayce, all are documented at his foundation known as the ARE (Association of Research and Enlightenment) P O Box 595, Virginia Beach, Virginia. These readings constitute one of the largest and most amazing records of psychic ability known to the world.

According to Cayce, our mind is divided into three levels of consciousness. The conscious mind is the storehouse of information that we consciously know, the mind we use for our everyday life. The next level of mind is our subconscious, and Cayce tells us in the deeper level of this mind "what is known to one subconscious mind is known to another, whether conscious of the fact or not." This theory that all minds can somehow contact one another on a subconscious level is compatible to Jung's idea of the Collective Unconscious. This ability to subconsciously be able to communicate could be an explanation for the existence of ESP and psychic abilities. If we can use this universal knowledge which is based in the deeper levels of our subconscious mind, we theoretically could know things that would seem impossible for us to know. According to Cayce, we all have access to this knowledge.

The third layer of our mind is the superconscious. This is the spark of God which is within each and everyone of us. It is our connection to God . . . an awareness of the soul . . . and it is eternal. Jung calls the great pool of unconscious memories of all people the Collective Unconscious, but Cayce labels it the "Akashic Records" or "The Book of Life." Within this Book of Life is recorded all deeds and thoughts of all mankind throughout the ages, and is not limited to this world, but is universal. Those who are attuned to the superconscious mind within themselves, can tap into the Akashic Record, and Cayce's psychic gifts came from his ability to lay aside his conscious mind and enter the realm of the superconscious. We each have untapped psychic ability, and with work, could tap into this superconscious state. According to Cayce, psychic ability is an attribute of the soul, thus we all have this hidden potential.

Cayce explains how, at death, the subconscious mind takes over the work of the conscious mind, which is now set aside. Death is only a change in consciousness. If this is true, then those who experience near-death theoretically are now working from a subconscious level and have access to the Collective Unconscious. Through this pool of knowledge, they cannot only communicate with those who are deceased, but can visit other realms of existence. This, of course, would also explain how many bereaved individuals receive dream visits from loved ones who have died. While we are in the dream state, we are using the subconscious level of our mind, and if those who are deceased are also on that level, then it is logical to assume they both are able to communicate through the Collective Unconscious.

Bernie Siegel, M.D. is a practicing surgeon in New Haven and also teaches at Yale University. In his best-seller, *Love, Medicine, and Miracles*, Siegel tells us, "There are hidden channels of communication from the unconscious to our conscious minds." When speaking of spiritual guidance in relation to this channel of communication, Siegel says,

> Choosing spiritual guidance also helps you to see that people's minds and souls are interconnected in ways normally obscured from our everyday vision. The separateness most of us experience is illusory, and seeing through it makes life even more meaningful. Botanist Rupert Sheldrake has recently proposed "morphoegenetic fields" as a means of communication to explain the otherwise baffling results of certain experiments. It seems that, once rats in one laboratory have learned a particu-

lar maze, other rats anywhere in the world, having had no contact with the original rats, learn that same maze faster. Apparently, once a thought has been thought, it can be
communicated to others. Sheldrake believes this may be the
reason why an important discovery is often made simultaneously by several people working independently in different
areas of the world.

In an introductory foreword to *The Tibetan Book of the Dead*, Lama
Anagarika Govinda explains how, through concentration and other yo-
gic practices, some people are able to bring the subconscious into the
realm of the conscious. When they do this, they draw upon "the unre-
stricted treasury of subconscious memory, wherein are stored the records
not only of our past lives but the records of the past of our race, the past
of humanity, and of all pre-human forms of life, if not of the very consciousness that makes life possible in this universe."

Betty Eadie, in her book *Embraced By The Light*, presents an interesting twist to the idea of the unconscious. While having an extended
NDE, Eadie collected a vast amount of fascinating universal knowledge,
some of which was about our unconscious mind. She says,

I learned that all thoughts and experiences in our lives are recorded in our subconscious minds. They are also recorded in
our cells, so that, not only is each cell imprinted with a genetic coding, it is also imprinted with every experience we
have ever had. Further, I understood that these memories are
passed down through the genetic coding to our children.
These memories then account for many of the passed on
traits in families, such as addictive tendencies, fears,
strengths, and so on.

If Eadie's information is true, there may be a possibility that our ability
to connect with the Collective Unconscious may come through our
DNA!

In chapter one, I explained how most visions of the bereaved occur
when one is in the hypnagogic state. This is an altered state of consciousness which occurs when you are half awake or half asleep . . . just
falling off, or just waking up. Edgar Cayce labeled this the "twilight." If
you have ever read a book about dream interpretation, you will know
that dream experts tell you in order to better remember your dreams
you should not wake to an alarm, but wake up slowly and calmly. If you
do this, you will be in the hypnagogic state, balanced between con-

scious and subconscious mind. You are now able to retrieve information from the subconscious level while still being partially conscious. Understanding the workings of this state will greatly assist you in the comprehension of the visions of the bereaved. If the deceased and the living are both in the subconscious state, they will now be able to communicate via the Collective Unconscious.

Being out of the body also enables us to experience altered states of consciousness as well as other dimensions of existence. The near-deather tells us how he leaves his physical body, and can actually turn around and see it lying there. Those who experience near-death, however, are not the only ones to have an out-of-body experience. There are many parapsychological scientists who have studied the out-of-body experience (sometimes referred to as astral travel). Studies have shown three out of ten people will have an OBE (out-of-body experience) sometime during their life.

Among the many who have studied this phenomena is Robert Monroe, the founder of a private institution devoted to the study of the OBE. In the 1950's, Mr. Monroe began to have spontaneous out-of-body experiences. At first he was overwhelmed and feared he may be going insane, but eventually he was curious enough to begin a systematic study of the phenomena. Because he was not ingrained in a specific belief system, he was able to keep an open mind and pursue the study with a scientific approach.

He and the hundreds of others who have attended his institute now do not "believe" in the ability of the individual mind to survive without the body, but "know" that it exists through actual experience.

According to Monroe there are several interesting aspects of being out-of-body:

1. You perceive yourself as separated from your physical body but you think and act the same.
2. You keep the shape of your physical body, but the more familiar you are with out-of-body travel, the more liquid you become. This second body is somehow "plastic" and changeable, but you are "still you".
3. You are connected to your physical body by an invisible cord. (Many metaphysical writings tell us that our soul is connected to our body by a silver cord, which breaks at the moment of death. This idea is even mentioned in the Bible: Ecclesiastics, Chapter 12, Verses 6 & 7).
4. When out-of-body there is no deceit, for all of what we are is "up front" and open. (This also agrees with metaphysical teachings)

5. You may visit a recently deceased love one when in an out-of-body state. This can be accomplished by just thinking of them.
6. You can go anywhere in time...past, present, or future. (Those who have had an NDE also tell us that the other side is timeless).
7. When out-of-body we are part of another energy system that co-mingles with the physical life on earth.

According to Monroe, "OBE's have been related to the sleep state and thus dismissed as simply dreams—except that they do not fit the hazy and unreal quality associated with dreaming." I can personally attest to this fact because I have found it to be true when I had my own OBE.

At the Monroe Institute, built in the 1970's, Monroe and his associates continue to study the OBE and various aspects of human consciousness. Thousands of people have come to the institute and experienced the evolving program known as "Gateway Voyage." If you would like further information about Monroe and his institute please write to:

> The Monroe Institute
> Route 1, Box 175
> Faber, Virginia 22938

In his book, *A Practical Guide To Death and Dying*, John White has the following to say about the OBE,

> Ekstasy is the ancient Greek word from which the English "ecstasy" comes. Ordinarily we understand ecstasy to mean some delightful emotional state . . . rapture, perhaps, or swooning. It means "to stand outside of," to be outside of your normal everyday sense of self. In its original meaning, however, it denoted out-of-body experience (OBE). Ex, out of, and status, a fixed or static condition, is the ancient way of describing "flight of the soul" or astral projection . . . the experience in which you find your consciousness or your center of self-awareness floating in space exterior to your physical body. In the OBE condition, you are fully and normally conscious. That is, you know you are not dreaming or fantasizing. Also, you perceive some portion of your environment which could not possibly be perceived from where your physical body is at the time. You are truly, literally, "outside yourself."

White continues by explaining how people who have experienced an OBE are convinced they will survive death. The experience is almost like a rehearsal for the real thing. Just as reincarnation shows us how the human personality can transcend time, the OBE demonstrates that our consciousness can also transcend space.

In the summer of 1993, I attended a workshop on out-of-body experiences with Rick Stack, author of *Out-of-Body Adventures*. I learned that 10 to 15 percent of the general population will have at least one OBE in their lifetime. These experiences are usually involuntary, and occur when one is in shock, pain, near death, tired, stressful, asleep, in meditation, under anesthesia or in a totally relaxed state. The OBE has been reported by all cultures at all times in history. While having an OBE, you can not only go wherever you wish in the physical world, but can also visit other dimensions. According to Stack, while in this state you can visit with deceased relatives as well as travel through time.

Stack explained how most of us experience the out-of-body state while we are asleep, but don't remember it. Many times these experiences are confused and intertwined with our dreams because we usually jump into an OBE while having a dream, and when we return to the body we also must go through that same dream state. Dreams can be confusing and full of symbology, and no matter how clear and precise the OBE may be, we still have to pass through the dream state to return to our body. This explains the confusion. If we are lucky, and remain lucid (are consciously aware we are dreaming) during the dream state, we can effectively remember the OBE. I believe the reason why I was so successful in having an OBE visit with my son is because I have been recording and studying my dreams for many years and can remain lucid during the dream state.

Mark Thurston, Ph.D., author of *Dreams, Tonight's Answers for Tomorrow's Questions*, devotes an entire chapter of his book to the OBE. Thurston explains how many OBE's occur while one is having a "lucid" dream. Simply put, a dream becomes lucid when you KNOW you are dreaming while the dream is happening. These lucid dreams are usually extremely vivid and real and are "dramatically different from a normal dream."

According to Dr. Thurston, lucid dreaming and astral travel (OBE) usually go hand and hand. During an OBE, our spiritual body (sometimes called our astral or etheric body) leaves the physical one. This spiritual body is composed of higher forms of energy and vibrates at a higher level than do our physical bodies.

Thurston explains how Kirlian photography, a form of electrophotography, shows an invisible energy surrounding the physical body. This energy field actually shows up on the film. This energy body interpenetrates the physical one, but at night when we sleep, the spiritual energy body can leave the physical one and either travels around the physical world, or goes into other realms of existence. Even though this happens frequently, we never remember it except when we are having a lucid dream.

Thurston tells us that it is possible to visit with deceased friends or relatives while visiting the other realms of existence in an OBE. But Thurston warns if you keep trying to visit the dead through OBE's you can hold them back from their progress on the other side. The OBE can be spiritually revitalizing and can give us an exhilaration that carries over into our daily living. We can also discover our own spirituality. He says:

> We see directly that we are citizens of an immense universe that extends not just to the far reaches of outer space, but to the limitless potential of inner space.
>
> Lest we misunderstand what these dreams of power come to teach us, let's remember this fundamental law of spiritual growth: 'Everything we seek can be found within.' Even the astral dimension is within ourselves. Our objective should not be to see how far out of the body we can go. Instead, it is to see how much love and wisdom we can bring into the body.

The book *The Link* is a story about an English psychic named Matthew Manning. As a teen, Manning was able to willingly leave his physical body. He tells how one day, at boarding school, he left his body lying on the bed in the dormitory while his consciousness went home. Upon arrival at his house, Manning followed his mother around as she completed her household chores. As he did this, she kept stopping her work and looking behind her. She would look directly at him, yet not see him. Manning explains:

> I later questioned her about this occasion, and we exchanged both sides of our experience. She had not seen me, but she had "felt" that I was in the house on that morning; she had the feeling that I was standing behind her, watching her while she was in the kitchen. She had walked around the house looking for me, and was half expecting to see me.

I find this story fascinating because it shows how a mother can have the "feeling of the presence" from someone who is not actually physically dead. If Manning came to visit her in his astral or spiritual body, and he was not dead, can we then logically assume the astral body is the same in death as it is in life, still maintaining the same personality? In both cases the spiritual body functions quite well without the physical one, and is strong enough to make someone feel its presence.

The person who has had an OBE knows that he will survive death, for he has experienced how it feels to exist separately from his human body. Dr. Elisabeth Kubler-Ross, the world-famous expert on death and dying, has a collection of hundreds of cases of OBE's from around the world. In her book, *On Life After Death*, she explains that no one should fear death because at that moment, we are never alone. From the stories of her many patients, she is convinced each of us has a spirit guide (or guardian angel) that is there for us at the moment of death. This moment brings painlessness, calmness, and joy. In her experience, young children who are dying slowing from cancer acquire the ability to leave their body and travel around at will. During these trips, they meet spirit guides and loved ones who have previously died. These short trips help them with their transition as they become familiarized with their upcoming state of existence.

Kubler-Ross explains how all of us have OBE's during certain stages of sleep, but most of us are not consciously aware of them. She has this to say about those who have experienced being out-of-body:

> They all share the same common denominator. They are all fully aware of shedding their physical body, and death, as we understand it in scientific language, does not really exist. Death is simply a shedding of the physical body like the butterfly shedding its cocoon. It is a transition to a higher state of consciousness where you continue to perceive, to understand, to laugh, and to be able to grow. The only thing you lose is something that you don't need anymore, your physical body. It's like putting away your winter coat when spring comes, you know that the coat is shabby and you don't want to wear it anymore. That's virtually what death is all about. Not one of the patients who has had an OBE was ever again afraid to die. Not one of them.

CHAPTER THREE

MY STORY

At approximately 1:30 A.M. on the morning of May 24, 1991, the ringing of the phone awoke me from a sound sleep.

"Hello. Is this Kay Woods?"

'Yes, it is."

"Are you the mother of Andy Woods."

"Yes, I am."

"There has been an accident. Come to the Emergency Room of the hospital immediately."

"Was my son in an accident?"

"Yes.'"

"Was he seriously injured?"

"I cannot say at this time. Please come to the hospital."

"Come on! Is he seriously injured?"

"Yes. Please come immediately."

This is the living nightmare that all parents of teenagers dread, and I lived it. I threw on some clothes and headed toward the hospital. On the way my thoughts ran wild. *Oh, please God, please. Let him be O.K. I'll do anything you want, just let him be O.K.*

It was Memorial Day weekend. My 7 year old daughter, Katie, was at her Grandparents. My 16 year old son, Andy, was at an overnight party at a friend's farm out in the country. I walked him to the car about 9:30 that evening. He went with two other friends in an old V.W. Beetle. I knew where they were going and totally trusted them. Approximately one half hour later, on the way to the party, the car slid on a rainy roadway while making a turn and ran into a tree. As the police and ambulance cleared up the wreckage and took the boys to the hospital, I slept peacefully. How could I have not known? How could I have slept right through it? Two boys were declared dead at the scene, having died upon impact. The driver survived.

When I arrived at the hospital, I was greeted by the patient advocate.

"I am Mrs. Woods. I'm here to see my son, Andy."

"Wait a minute, and I'll get the doctor."

"I want to see my son now! Why can't I see him now?"

"Wait here, please, and I'll get the doctor."

It was at that moment that I knew the worst. This man didn't want to be the one to give me the bad news, he would let the doctor do that. The doctor turned out to be the coroner (thank God I didn't know that at the time).

"I want to see my son, Andy. Please take me to him now." The feelings of dread and panic were creeping up my spine like a bad dream coming true.

"I'm sorry, Mrs. Woods, but your son was a fatality in this accident."

I laughed and said, "You're kidding."

"No, Mrs. Woods, come and sit down."

Oh God, Oh God, no. NO! My baby. My baby boy!

I heard myself calmly say, "I'm going to need a tranquilizer and an antacid (My stomach had already begun to pump out acid at an alarming rate)." After I took the pills, I calmly went to the phone to call friends and family. I was like a zombie in a trance and just automatically did what I had to do. I was in what the professional would call the initial stage of grief, "shock and denial."

And so the story goes for those of us who lose their children. I didn't realize how, every year, many thousands of people experience the death of a child until this happened to me. How does a parent who loses a beloved child cope with the loss? Many of us don't, and it eventually ruins our lives. Others learn to live with it, accept it, and go on.

I was lucky. I had a strong background in Metaphysics and had read many books about the near-death experience and the afterlife. Through my extensive reading, I had a pretty good idea of what happens to us when we die.

Fate had it that I was already in the process of completing a Master's Degree in Transpersonal Psychology, specializing in bereavement. I had a pretty good handle on what grief was and how the average person reacts to it. Now I was going to get the lesson first hand, whether I wanted it or not.

Many people ask me, "How did you live through it, and not go insane? How do you bear it?" The unexplained and paranormal events surround Andy's death helped me to live through the tragedy and go on with my life.

After spending the first dreadful night with friends and family, I finally tried to lay down for some much needed rest the following afternoon. I awoke startled from this nap with an overwhelming vision of Andy's smiling radiant face. He was surrounded by a brilliant white light and looked remarkably peaceful, serene, and wonderful. I lay there awhile thinking about what had just happened. Had it really been Andy? Was he trying to let me know that everything was O.K.?

That Memorial Day weekend was the longest in my life. I had to wait until Tuesday for the funeral. The house was buzzing with friends and family, all in a scurry of activity. I was numb. On the Monday before the funeral, I started to look through Andy's writing in order to find something that might be appropriate to read at the funeral. Andy was an avid writer of short stories, poems, and musical lyrics. I came across the following poem:

ENJOY THE SHOW

I can see so clearly now, clearer than I've ever seen before.
And if you search the darkest corridors, you'll find a single door.

You turn the beautiful shiny doorknob, feeling a pain that's somewhat sharp.
And opening it slowly, you'll hear the slow echo of the angel's harp.

I can taste the air now, I could never seem to taste the air before.
And if you swim the deepest depths, the waves will lead you to the sparkling shore.

And grasping through the grains of sand, they'll fall through your fingertips.
And the tides tend to taste bitter as they stream into your lips.

Everything I hear is so much louder now, it was never this loud before.
You may have to search your life away, but you'll know when you need to search no more.

You'll find a place where colors are bright and like waters they swirl.
The straightest of lines will make a slow and wonderful curl.

I can feel so perfectly now, nothing has ever been this perfect before.
Searching through the vastness and the black, you'll find the sun's inner core.

Where your life is so bright, that beauty will be all you know.
And you can sit back relax and enjoy the show.

Sit back, relax and enjoy the show.
The world turns on and you stay fresh and new.

You can never die, time just lets you go.
Until you search you'll never know, what your mind can do.

ANDY WOODS - 1991

I later found out from his friends that he had been working on this poem a week before the accident and had just completed it. I asked myself, "Did Andy somehow know on a soul level that it was his time to die?" At that time I was not sure. After years of research, however, I am sure. Those who have a near-death experience tell us that while they are on the "other side" they are told to go back for it is "not their time." I believe it was Andy's time, and on some level he was aware of it.

When my phone bill came later that month, I discovered that he had made $100 worth of long distance calls. Andy never made a long-distance call without my permission. It was something he wouldn't have even considered. If he knew he was going to die somewhere on a soul level, did he spend the month saying good-bye to friends he knew he would never see again?

About a week before the accident I ran into Andy on the stairs of our home . . . he was going up, I was going down. He stopped and looked at me, gave me a big hug and said, "I love you, Mom. You know I appreciate everything you have done for me." I answered, "I love you too, Hon. Now what is it you want? Money? Clothes?" We laughed together. Little did I realize this was his last chance to say good-bye and "I love you."

After the horror of the funeral, life calmed down to a dark, dreadful concession of continuing black days of misery. Two weeks had passed when I had the following vivid dream:

I was sitting in someone's living room. I looked up and Andy was standing there. I immediately knew that it was Andy's spirit. I said, "I wondered when you were going to show up." He came over and took both my hands and we flew upward into a star-filled night sky. We flew through some kind of a force field because I had a strange feeling of suction when we passed through it. I remember thinking to myself that when we went through that force field we were probably on "the other side."

We flew around the night sky as the stars and milky way shown the way. When we came back down he said to me, "You know, Mom, I can't keep doing this." I knew that he must go on to do his soul's work, and I must, in turn, stay here on earth to do mine. He told me he had a duty to watch over three little girls on earth. Their mother slept in late and there was no one to watch them in the morning. The girls were in danger, especially the youngest. It was his job to watch over them and keep them safe.

I can't remember the rest of the visit except for the end. I told him I didn't want to go back, I wanted to stay there with him. He answered,

"Mom, you're here till you're 71." Since that time, I truly believe I will die at age 71. Sometimes I wonder if I actually WILL die at that age, or maybe it will become a self-fulfilled prophecy. It will be interesting to find out. One thing I do know . . . with every birthday that passes, I no longer fear getting a year older, but look at it as a countdown to when I get to see Andy again. This really does make aging a lot easier!

I awoke from this dream with an incredible sense of peace. This was not like a regular dream. It was extremely vivid and I was lucid the whole time. When one is lucid during a dream, they know they are dreaming while they are in the dream. I can distinguish it from other dreams I have had of Andy because in a regular dream, Andy is alive again or has never really died at all. In this dream I immediately knew I was in the presence of Andy's spiritual or "astral" body.

Another interesting incident happened several weeks after Andy's passing. My daughter Katie, who was seven at the time, came up to me and said, 'Do you know what, Mommy? Andy's guardian angel came and got his spirit before the car ever hit the tree." When I asked her where she heard such a thing, she shrugged her shoulders and answered, "I don't know, Mommy, it's just something I know." Out of the mouths of babes.

A STRANGE VISIT

About six weeks after Andy's death, I was at my lowest point in grieving. I was very depressed and overwhelmed with sorrow. On Father's Day, my family took my father out to brunch, but I wouldn't go. Everyone was concerned about leaving me alone because it was the first time I was alone since the death. I insisted on staying alone, however. What everyone else DIDN'T know was I was on the brink of "losing it."

A knock came to the door. It was a young man who looked to be in about his early 20's. He had a Bible in his hand. I remember thinking, *Just what I need . . . a Bible thumper. He is probably using Andy's death as an excuse to try to get me to join his church!*

He looked at me and said, "Are you the mother of Andy, the boy who was killed?" I answered yes, VERY skeptically. He continued, "Please, listen to me. I had a vision about your son last night. Please don't slam the door on my face. This is very important." I reluctantly invited him to sit with me on the front porch. He said, "Last night the youth group at my church was looking through this yearbook. I was paging through it and when I came to a picture of this boy, I immediately began to cry and said to the others: something is wrong with this boy in the picture. One of the kids said, "That is Andy Woods. He was killed in an auto accident a few weeks ago." Then I saw a vision of you standing in your kitchen (he later described to me what my kitchen looked like) and I heard a voice say, "Everything is OK with the son, but not so with the mother. If you don't get to her and tell her to keep her faith in God, she will have a nervous breakdown by the end of the week."

He told me he was planning to come and see me sometime in the middle of the week, but when he was sitting in church that morning, the same voice said to him "Go and see her NOW." So he got up in the middle of the service and came to see me. The ironic part of this whole thing was that he arrived about three minutes after my family left and then left the house about one minute before they returned.

He explained that the voice told him to tell me there are loving arms around me at all times and to keep my faith in God. We chatted together for about an hour. He wanted nothing from me . . . not to join his church, not to give him money . . . nothing. He explained that this kind of thing happens to him often and many times people slam the door on his face or tell him to go away. I believe it must be difficult for a young man of that age to have the responsibility of such visions.

When my sister pulled up in front of the house and got out of the car, I ran up to her and said, "Do you see that young man getting into his car up the street?" She did. "Good, I continued, I just wanted to make sure he wasn't an angel or something."

I continued to occasionally hear from this young man in the year following Andy's death. He would call or write to tell me he was thinking of me, and we would have a nice chat. I believe he was divinely sent to me in the hour of my greatest need.

THE GIFT OF SONG

During the first few months after Andy's death I would often wake up with songs in my head. I would find myself humming them in the morning, and when I thought about the words of the song, they seemed to have special meaning . . .

"Take my hand. I'm a stranger in paradise. Alone in a wonderland. A stranger in paradise."

"Where do I begin to tell the story of how great a love can be . . . to tell the story that is older than the sea."

"My heart will be blessed with the sound of music . . . and I'll sing once more . . . " (when I received this song I remember thinking: Will I ever be well enough to want to sing again? I believe Andy was telling me that I will be able to sing once more.)

"Johnny Angel, how I love him. How I tingle when he holds me tight . . . and together we will know how lovely heaven can be." (Andy's first name is John).

"When you walk through a storm, keep your head up high. And don't be afraid of the night. At the end of the road is a golden sun, and the sweet silver song of a lark. Hold on through the wind, hold on through the rain, though your dreams be torn and dark. Walk on, walk on with hope in your heart and you'll never walk alone. You'll never walk alone...

"When will our eyes meet? When will I touch you? When will this strong yearning end? And when will I hold you again?"

I never quite understood why Andy always sent me these songs until one day when I was going through his writings I found this poem . . .

I can't see you as we sit here in the depths of dark.
But I know you're here all the same,
I feel you in my heart.

And I know the thoughts that trouble you,
I know the tears you cry.
But we all must face some grounded life
between the times we fly.

Everything will turn out fine,
You know it can and will.
But until the time we smile and die,
We've got some time to kill.

So sit down and sing a song with me,
it doesn't matter which one.
I'll pull you through the pain with me
Until the night is done.

(You are unstoppable. The river flows inside of you)

Andy Woods 1991

"So sing a little song with me. It doesn't matter which one.
I'll take you through the pain with me until the night is done."
What a gift I had just received!

THE BEREAVEMENT COUNSELOR

Several weeks after Andy's death, I decided to go and see a bereavement counselor to help work out my feelings. I checked the bulletin board of the local metaphysical book store to see if I could find some kind of a counselor, and I found a card saying "Sherry Bear, Bereavement Counselor."

I called her and made an appointment. She didn't have an office, so we met at her home and sat outside at the picnic table. We talked about Andy for about an hour, and I shared how much I missed him and loved him. In the middle of a sentence, she interrupted me and said, "Wait a minute, I'm getting something." I didn't know what she meant at first, but then she began to talk . . . "I can see Andy and his friend Mikey. They want you to know that there was no pain in their time of passing." (I was shocked, this woman must be a psychic!) She continued . . . "I see Andy. Who is the pretty little dark-haired girl he's with? He's holding her hand. Oh! it's his sister. She has the prettiest blue-gray eyes." By this time I was in tears. This woman did not know me from Adam. There was no way for her to know I had a baby daughter who had died when she was 12 days old or that her Daddy had blue-gray eyes. Then she spoke of a fuzzy little dog who was with them. I had a Yorkshire Terrier who had died about four years before.

Those of you who are skeptics may say that she just researched information about me so I would keep coming back, and she could make more money. This, however, is not the case for she continued to see me for about one year and never charged me a cent!

She continued. "I see fire." I immediately thought of Mikey, who had died with Andy, because there were bonfires at all of Mikey's parties at the farm and for a farewell to Mikey, his family had a final bonfire into which they threw Mikey's ashes. She went on, "I'm getting the name Danny. Who is Danny?" "I don't know any Danny," I told her. "Don't worry, she answered, it will turn up."

When I got home, I called Mikey's Mom to let her know what had happened and share the message from the boys which said they had no pain in passing. She was glad to hear this and at the end of the conversation with her I asked if the boys had a friend named Danny down at the farm that I didn't know about. The name Danny came up quite strongly. Mikey's Mom began to say, "Oh My God! Oh My

God!" "What's wrong," I interrupted. "Mikey's Uncle Danny helped me to raise him when he was a baby. He passed away several years ago."

So the boys are with Uncle Danny. This confirms what the near-death experience tells us. When we get to the Light, our deceased loved ones are waiting for us. Speaking with Mikey's mother was the confirmation I needed to make me truly believe the counselor was the "Real McCoy." How could she have known about Danny? She certainly didn't pick my brain for that name, because I didn't know it!

Please don't run to the nearest psychic because of my experience. Finding a reputable psychic is a difficult business. Just as any one else who does public service, some are very good . . . very honest. Some are out for one thing . . . your money. Through my readings I have found that most reputable psychics will recommend trying contact only about once a year. The continuing attempt to try to reach a deceased loved one will hold him back from his progress and life on the other side.

Words cannot express the comfort that woman gave me. There is no monetary value I could put on this information. It gave me the peace and understanding that Andy was fine and was with his little sister and his dog. I would see them both again in the Light and they would wait for me together until I got there.

I continued to see Sherry for about a year. Sometimes she gave me messages, sometimes not. Mostly not. We talked about me, my emotions, feelings, expectations, and plans for the future.

My most profound experience occurred about six months after Andy's death. While sleeping, I had an out-of-body experience in which I rose up through the roof of my house into the evening sky. I remember being able to see what it looked like between the ceiling of my bedroom and the floor of my attic. It was winter and I was surprised I wasn't cold. Then I proceeded through space at what seemed to be faster than the speed of light, but I was not in the least bit frightened. I could see the lights of the stars and planets as I zoomed by them. I found myself in a large room where people were eating at long tables. Among them was my maternal grandmother who had died several years before. I was pleased and surprised to see her and excitedly said, "Grandma, How are you? I'm so glad to see you!" She calmly answered, "Why I'm fine," in a manner as if to say "What's all the fuss about?" I remember being surprised at her appearance because when she died she was 96 and had snow white hair. She now appeared to be about forty with dark hair and those old "Cat's Eye" glasses from the 1950's.

After a short chat with Grandma, the details of which I don't remember, I proceeded to go to look for Andy, and traveled through various hallways in search for him. I finally found myself in a vacant lot that appeared to be in the inner city. I thought to myself, *This is supposed to*

be heaven, why the inner city environment? Why the run-down buildings?
Then I remembered how I had read somewhere that in the Astral World
we find ourselves in the environment we are most comfortable. There
was a sandlot ball game going on in this vacant lot with mostly Black
and Hispanic children. Again, I though to myself, *Everyone thinks these
kids are dead, and they're up here playing ball.*

I looked on the pitcher's mound and there was my Andy. His hair
was longer than it was when he died and he appeared to be taller and
more muscular. He looked great and his eyes sparkled like the stars! I
watched the game for a while, and then he came over to speak to me.
We had a lovely visit, most of which I do not recall. I was thrilled to be
there with him. When I asked him, "Where are we? Where is this
place?," he calmly put his hand through a nearby wall and said, "I'm
right here, Mom, you just can't see me."

Another aspect of the dream I find interesting is how I remember
looking down and seeing broken glass under my feet. I was concerned
about cutting myself, but Andy said to me, "We're in spirit Mom, the
glass can't hurt you." (I was later told by Sherry that the glass was probably a symbol of breaking through from one dimension to another).

I do not remember returning to my bed or saying good-bye to
Andy, but remembered the dream and all of its detail upon waking that
morning. I cannot explain this experience in earthly terms. There are no
sufficient words. Many of the "experts" would tell me that it was a vivid
dream brought on by my longing to be with Andy. The only explanation I can give is that the people who experience near-death know they
are not hallucinating, and I know I was not just dreaming!

THE FEELING OF THE PRESENCE

Approximately 3 months after Andy's death, I was alone in my antique
shop ironing a vintage dress when I found myself singing a song: "Lean
on me when you're not strong. I'll be your strength, I'll help you carry
on. Lean on me." Suddenly, the memory of Andy was extremely vivid
to me, as if I could still actually see him. I had my back to the entrance
of the shop and I felt as though someone had come in the door. I
looked around, but no one was there. I continued to iron and this time
I felt the presence of someone in the shop again. Someone was standing
right behind me at my right shoulder. I could feel them so closely, I
should have been able to hear them breathing in my ear. I turned suddenly because I was alone in the shop and I felt as though someone had
sneaked up behind me. As I turned again, I realized no one was there. It
was at this moment I realized I was experiencing a visit from Andy.

It's interesting, but this actually frightened me. I don't know why, maybe because I was alone. It wouldn't seem logical that anything to do with Andy would be frightening to me, but it was. I said aloud, "Andy you're scaring me. Try to visit again when I'm more together." At once he went away. I was amazed how this occurrence frightened me. Most people I have talked to or read about who have had these experiences found them to be full of love and peace and not at all frightening.

AN ANGEL MEDITATION

While attending a metaphysical seminar at Kutztown University, I had the privilege of taking a workshop with Janie Howard, author of *Commune With The Angels*. During this workshop, she led us through a guided meditation to meet with deceased loved ones. She played the most beautiful music: Andrew Lloyd Weber's "Pie Jesu." She explained to us she had been informed by her angels that this particular piece of music had a special vibration and was good for meditation. As I listened to the music and Janie's words, I found myself with Andy. The music was very sad, and I was crying. He took me into his arms and we danced together. Then he led me deep inside of my own body and, as I watched, he took a thread and sewed up my broken heart. When I awoke from the meditation, I was sobbing, but felt cleansed inside. Thank you, Janie!

A CHRISTMAS VISIT

About two weeks before Christmas in the year of Andy's death, I was awakened about 5:00 A.M. by the television. The TV turned itself on and said "Merry Christmas!" and then turned itself off again. Many people have said to me, "You must have rolled over onto the remote." But the remote was on top of the TV. I know there are many people who would never believe this was a message from Andy, but I did at the time. I sat up in bed and said, "Merry Christmas to you, too, Andy. I love you!" After years of research, I realize that TV's and radios turning off and on by themselves is a common occurrence in the house of the bereaved!

I know my personal story sounds so incredible that some of you will believe it is fiction. Believe me, it is not. For those of you who have had such experiences, hearing my story will only confirm the reality of them. To the non-believer, I can only say unless you personally have such an experience, you will probably NEVER believe me. My purpose is to assist those who have had such experiences or may have them in the future.

THE DREAM VISIT

Man has recognized the importance of dreams since ancient times. In the book *Working With Dreams,* authors Ullman and Zimmerman present an extensive history of the dream experience. One of the first written works on dreams is called the Chester Beatty papyrus. This Egyptian book is dated somewhere around 2,000 B.C. According to the ancient Egyptians, dreams were messages from the gods in which man was assisted and informed. The ancient Jews also believed dreams to be messages of guidance from their God, Yahweh. According to legend, The Koran (the holy book of Islam) was given to Mohammed in a dream. It is reported that every morning after prayers, Mohammed asked each of his disciples what they had dreamed.

The ancient Greeks used dreams as a means of healing, and erected dream temples in various locations throughout their country. The sick would come to the temple, make sacrifices, engage in purification rites, and then go to sleep with the hope of being healed while in the dream state. Later in history, however, Aristotle stated that dreams were not messages from the gods, but came from one's own inner sensations.

The early Christian Church believed in the importance of dreams. Ullman and Zimmerman tell us about the beliefs of a few of the church's early leaders:

> Clement was a Christian of the late second century in the Greek school. He believed that true dreams came from the soul's depth and revealed the relationship between man and God. He concluded that in sleep, the soul, freed from sense impressions, has a heightened ability to reflect on itself and come to a truer hold on reality.

For Augustine (354-430 A.D.) dreams were an important tool in grasping both the inner workings of the mind of man and his relationship with God. His own conversion was foretold in his mother's dream.

The medieval church taught that dreams were not from God and should be ignored, but by the end of the middle ages, Martin Luther believed dreams to be God's way of helping us recognize our own sins.

Although dreams seemed to go in and out of "fashion" throughout the course of history, in most instances they were held in high regard.

The first scientific study of the dream was completed by Freud with the presentation of his work *Interpretation of Dreams* in 1900. Jung, a contemporary of Freud, theorized that the dream could connect us to the Collective Unconscious. Ullman and Zimmerman state:

> Jung saw our dreams extending beyond the realm of the personal unconscious to tap into what he referred to as the "collective unconsciousness." He felt that the deepest layers of our unconscious harbored certain tendencies that were common to the human race. These predispositions were genetically determined responses to the critical events we all face in the course of our lives (birth, individuation, struggle with evil, and so on). These responses make their appearance in consciousness in the form of what he referred to as archetypal image.

As I explained in chapter two, when our mind is functioning on the subconscious level, we are able to "dip" into the great pool of knowledge called the Collective Unconscious. If, as Cayce describes, the subconscious mind takes over at the moment of death, then the deceased are also able to tap into this universal source. When we dream, our conscious mind sleeps, and our subconscious is in control. When both the living and the dead have access to the Collective Unconscious, communication is then possible. The dream visit is most likely the simplest way for us to visit with the deceased, which is probably why it is the most common form of communication.

According to Rosemary Guiley, *The Encyclopedia of Dreams*, dreams are not illusions, but as real as our waking consciousness, and when we are dreaming, the rules of space and time do not apply. She says:

> The fundamental wisdom about the reality of dreams has been understood and accepted universally since ancient times. The early Greeks and Romans, for example, believed that when the body was asleep, the soul became free to travel, especially to nonworldly, dreamlike realms wherein dwelled the lesser spirits who mediated between humans and the gods. Plato called this realm the "metaxu," or the "between." Here the human soul had experiences and encounters that had the same validity as experiences had during waking life. What made the dream experiences special, however, were their supernatural characteristics. In dreams, it was possible to meet the gods, to

see the future, and to be healed of illness and disease. Similarly, shamanic cultures have accessed the same alternate dreamlike reality for the same purposes.

Elsie Sechrist, in her book *Dreams, Your Magic Mirror*, explains how it is possible for the living to communicate with the dead:

> The dead differ from the living only in this respect: they are in a permanently subconscious state because the conscious mind of the physical body no longer exists. But the body is an expendable shell, and all else is intact. On the astral level of existence, the subconscious mind replaces the conscious mind of the soul, and the superconscious replaces the subconscious.

Hence, in dreams, we find that communication with those who have passed on is more logical than the average person is able to comprehend.

Sechrist explains how a woman who was having a reading asked Cayce about the conditions that make communication between subconscious states possible. The woman stated, "Is it our subconscious minds that meet, I in sleep and he in the cosmic (death) plane as a vibratory force meets a radio machine and causes a sound when the radio is turned on?" Cayce answered, "That is an illustration. Both minds must be in the same attunement or vibration and separated from the physical consciousness for these are of the spiritual consciousness. Only through an attunement may a message (from a departed one) be received."

In his book, *Edgar Cayce On Dreams*, Harman Bro, Ph.D. presents a chapter entitled "Dreams of the Living Dead." According to the Cayce readings, not only is dream communication between the deceased and the living a reality, but it is a frequent occurrence. While in an unconscious dream state, the dreamer can enter the "fourth dimension" of existence where he can meet with those who have died. Cayce sometimes called the place where the dead and the living meet "the Borderland."

Sometimes these meetings in the "Borderland" are for the sake of the living . . . to assure him all is well with the deceased, to give him advice from the other side, or to warn him of upcoming events. There are times, however, when the dream visit occurs for the sake of the "living dead." Bro states, "Sometimes the dead simply want to be known and recognized as still existent." Cayce stressed that it is not only the deceased who can help the living, but by our prayers and outpouring of love, we can also assist the dead. Cayce does warn, however, that constant attempts to communicate with the dead can hold him back from his intended journey.

When speaking of communication with the dead, Bro says:

> Sometimes it occurs because the dead want to show the living what death is like, to take away their fear and grief. Exploring the possible reality of such contact, one dreamer had her side pinched by a discarnate friend, so vividly that she screamed in fright, while another had his toe pulled when he asked for it . . . and did not ask again. One dream took a man inside the brain of a woman dying of cancer, a relative, and showed him precisely what a relief death was, when it finally came.

According to Cayce, when he has such a dream experience, the dreamer realizes that "the death state is more nearly a normal one for the soul than is earthly existence." We humans have it backwards. Instead of worrying about how much awareness we take with us into death, we should worry about how much spiritual awareness we take into life! To our eternal spiritual beings, the death state is actually more normal than being in a physical body. Bro tells us the deceased enjoy teaching the living and work directly with us when we pursue worthy causes. If a soul is well developed, he can see and understand better than the living and is in a position to give helpful guidance in many phases of life . . . health, finances, social causes, and relationships. The following story tells of how a woman was assisted by her deceased father.

THE BROWN ENVELOPE TIED WITH STRING

A Pennsylvania woman told me this heart-warming story about how her father reached from beyond the grave to help her in her time of need.

The mere fact that my parent's long-time home had to be sold was quite upsetting to both my sister and me. Going through all the memorable things that had accumulated over more than 35 years was not only painful, but overwhelming.

Our house had actually been sold immediately. The buyers had their eyes on our lovely white brick Cape Cod home for many years. When they heard it was on the market, they did not hesitate to proceed with the proper channels to put a bid on their dream house.

The evening before the final settlement was to transpire, my sister received a disturbing phone call from the realtor stating they could not locate the actual paper work which would indicate that the house had been paid off years ago.

My sister frantically phoned to inform me of this final blow we had to endure in selling our beloved home. We both knew we could not ask our dear Mother who was then living in a nursing home totally unable to communicate due to a devastating brain degeneration. Our father had died ten years prior to the onset of Mother's illness.

We both reassured one another that our Dad had always paid his bills on time. Recalling his announcement some twenty plus years ago that the house was finally paid off reinforced any uncertainties that the proof of payment did exist, but where?

For months and even years, though less frequently, I would dream of my father after his death. In my most vivid dreams, he would always be healed of the cancer that took his life. I would wake in the morning feeling comforted that I saw and spoke to my Dad once again.

On this tormenting evening of the lost deed, I went to bed feeling upset and confused. Questions raced in my head; had my sister and I inadvertently thrown away these very important documents? My father had kept excellent records over the years in an old desk. I can still visualize him sitting at his desk doing his "paper work" in an orderly fashion.

As I slept that stressful night, I had a dream. My Dad was again the healthy, vibrant, joking man I remember. He told me to look in the brown enveloped tied with string located in the bottom desk drawer. In the wee hours of the morning, I phoned my sister alerting her to where the missing papers might be located. Sure enough, there they were . . . in a brown envelope tied with string.

SURROUNDED BY LIGHT

Allen was killed by a drunk driver in 1986. His mother writes:

The day I buried my Allen, I "dreamt" or was visited by him. He was standing with a group of other children, surrounded on all sides with light. Allen was a leader, and he was in the front of the group, and all the children were wearing hats (Allen loved hats). But a smile was on his face, and I felt an extreme feeling of calmness come over me, because I knew, then, that he was in heaven, and he was O.K.

The next dream came during that awful six to eight months after, the reality time, when you constantly say, "How can it be he is not here?" Allen appeared at my bedside, and the room filled with light. We had a wonderful conversation about where he was. When I asked him how he liked heaven, he just said "It's all right." Then I said, but Allen, you are in the best place and he answered, "Oh, Mom, it is so beautiful, but I didn't want to make you feel bad." He was with another person, and he said "She is always with me." I looked over and from the back I saw a person with long loose clothing and long hair. Allen said he was in the best place where he knew all things. Before his death, Allen was an avid reader, and would read the dictionary before bedtime, so he could know all things . . . and now he did. He spoke about how he went through the tunnel in a go-cart (which is typical of him because he loved cars), and that he was with my aunt, whom he adored, and who died when he was only six years old. He also told me that he visits me often and watches me as I sleep. We then hugged and I kissed him and smelled him and felt him; it was the most amazing experience.!

Allen is not the only deceased loved one to appear with a friend who is unknown to the living. They seem to just come along for the ride! His mother must have found comfort in the fact that Allen was with his aunt. According to all of the after-death literature I have read, we are always reunited with our loved ones who have gone before. Those who have experienced "near death" tell us the same thing. As they are going into the light, they are greeted by loved ones who have gone before. I remember how in my first dream visit from my son, Andy, he, too, was surrounded by light. Like Andy, Allen also appeared to his mother with a group of children, maybe to let us know they are not alone. Allen is one of the only cases with whom I am familiar who told about his tunnel experience (as do those who have experienced an NDE).

Laura visited her mother in dream about three months after she died. Her mother tells this story:

STOP THAT CRYING

About three months after Laura died, I was asleep on my sofa. It was in the morning and I was really in that terribly painful state. Laura walked across the living room and sat down on the sofa across from me. When I saw her, I halfway sat up and just looked at her. She had on a bathrobe with a few rollers in her hair. When she sat down, she propped her legs up on the sofa, rested her arms across her knees, and put her head down on her knees and I couldn't really see her face. I was so overwhelmed at seeing her, I didn't say anything. She finally raised her head, and I could see her face. What a beautiful glowing face she had! What beauty I have never seen before! She said to me, "I only came to tell you to stop that crying and carrying on. I am all right." When she said that, I started to get up and go towards her. I wanted to touch her and hold her, but not so. She got up and moved away from me and as I followed her, she disappeared.

Many people who have dream visits tell us how the deceased tells them to stop crying and go on with their life. There are other sources which tell us how our inability to release those who have passed on may interfere with their soul's progression on the other side. A book that helped me better understand the importance of release is entitled

Arthur Ford Speaks From Beyond. Because of her psychic abilities, Eileen Sullivan was able to communicate with Ford after his death. Through Sullivan, Ford explains the existence in the afterlife. He dedicates the final chapter to those who grieve, and states that those who are deceased share our grief, but once they arrive in the other dimension, they realize that the time we spend apart is actually very short when compared to the time we spend in eternity. They sometimes feel sorry when they are unable to come to us and relieve our grief.

Many of us on earth think we will live our entire remaining life without our loved one. We sometimes believe this is the end, and we will never be together again. Ford states that our loved one has not gone anywhere, for there is nowhere to go. All dimensions are interspaced. He actually coexists in the same space. He adds we are never alone, but are always surrounded by the love of the deceased and their soul is always near. The more we grieve and refuse to go on with life without him, the harder it is for the deceased to adjust to his new surroundings. He states,

> Do not reproach yourself for things said or unsaid, promises not made that you wish had been made. None of this is necessary between two loving souls, for each knows the other. Those of us here look upon these things which cause you such grief as being superficial, for inside each soul is the true knowledge of God and God's ways and his goodness. The rest is unimportant by comparison. You will find your loved soul mate again and you will rejoice in the nearness of one to the other. You are never alone, for we are with you always.

Around the turn of the century, the yogi philosopher, Yogi Ramacharaka wrote his opinions on how we may influence the souls who have gone beyond. He believed the soul who hears the constant calls to return from his grieving loved ones will be kept from falling into a needed rest. He reports, "Our selfish grief and demands often cause our loved ones who have passed much pain, sorrow, and unrest." He then begs the griever to "let the soul depart in peace and take its well earned rest and gain its full development."

What he's basically saying here is that our inability to let go of the deceased will keep him from accomplishing what he wants to in the afterlife. Those who grieve should not fall into the trap of calling to and whining for this person the rest of their life. There is a time to grieve, and grieve we must (for without going through the grieving process, you will never heal), but not to the point that it will ruin the rest of our time on the planet. Our loved one wants us to go on with our life, and he will go on with his, and we will once again meet in the Light.

Mark Thurston, author of *Dreams, Tonight's Answers for Tomorrow's Questions*, tells us that Cayce's "Borderland" is the ream of consciousness in which a soul lives immediately after leaving the physical world. Through our dreams, we can enter into this Borderland. This kind of dream usually brings comfort, assistance, guidance, or help, and Thurston explains how these experiences can make the dreamer realize that love survives the grave.

When speaking of dream visits, however, Thurston warns, "It is better to let such experiences come spontaneously. Do not try to initiate them or force them. The loved one or friend in the Borderland is better able than you to see when such contact is useful and needed."

Elsie Sechrist's advice parallels that of Ford, Thurston, and Yogi Ramacharaka. She says, "Perhaps the most common dream experience in spirit communication is related to the message which in essence says, "I am fine and happy. Your grief, however is holding me back and making me sad. You can help me greatly by trying to overcome your sorrow. You must stop grieving!"

GOIN' FISHIN'

Wes died from a brain aneurysm at age ten. His mother tells this story.

A friend of mine, who I see usually twice a year called me on the phone and said, "I had a dream about Wes last night." She fell silent for a few seconds. Then she began again, through tears, saying that Wes came to her in a dream, and told her "Tell my Mom I'm going fishing with Poppa."

I began to cry tears of joy because my father, who had died in February, had always loved to fish with Wes when he came to our house. I asked my friend where Wes was when he came to her. She said she couldn't see his surroundings, only Wes standing in front of his poppa with a fishing pole in his hand. She told me the dream was so real to her that she sat up in bed and woke her husband, who encouraged her to tell me about it.

She wasn't sure if it would be too upsetting to me, but I assured her that it was very reassuring. One last thing. I asked her if she was aware of the fact that Wes called his grandpa "Poppa", and she said "No, I never knew that."

The term "evidential material" is sometimes used when someone receives information they previously didn't know from a person who is deceased. It is, therefore, believed to be evidence of real contact. This happened to me when I was told about Uncle Danny by the psychic when I had never heard about him before. This "proof" of contact also happened in the first dream about the envelope tied with string.

Why would our loved one contact someone other than us? This happens quite often, and I believe it is because our overwhelming sorrow and grief may in some way keep them from "getting through" to us. Why this happens in some cases and not in others, I don't know. Just the way some people are more susceptible to psychic experiences than others may explain why some of us have dream visits and others do not. It's as though some of us are better "radio receivers" than others, and the deceased looks around until he can find the best "receiver."

No one should ever feel guilty about not receiving a dream visit. I have met bereaved individuals who are longing for a dream visit, don't have one, and then somehow blame themselves for not being able to receive one. Self blame is never healthy, and this blame in itself may keep the bereaved from receiving the very thing he wants!

Harmon Bro, Ph.D. offers answers to the following question: When is one ready for dreams of the living dead?

> First of all, one is ready for such dreams when he has them. His subconscious will not feed him experiences he can't handle if he chooses to do so. Secondly, one is ready for dream contact with the dead when he will not speak lightly of them. In Cayce's view, such dreams could mean dangerous escapism.
>
> Thirdly, one is ready for dreams of the deead when he soundly loves and serves the living; such dreams always come for a personal reason, a personal growth of the dreamer, or some concrete service in the regular round of his daily life. Dream messages seeming to come for a general public are immediately suspect, for healthy contact with the dead was not designed to function for the living in this way.
>
> Fourthly, one is ready for dreams of the dead when he is as ready to give aid to the dead as to receive it. When prayer for a discarnate comes freely and naturally to mind, then visions of them may follow. Any other approach tends to be exploitative. Fifthly, one is ready for dreams of the dead loved one when he has worked through his griefs and guilts regarding them, and has forgiven them for hurts to himself. Lack of these makes a nearly impenetrable barrier.
>
> Finally, one may dream of the dead when his own full life draws to its natural close, and it is time for him to prepare for the next journey.

In the book *Regression Therapy*, Barbara Lamb offers her explanation as to why some of us receive visits and others do not:

The fact that some people are not aware of experiencing visits from deceased loved ones may be due either to the variance in people's receptivity to the phenomenon or to the variance in the "sending power" of the deceased. It takes intense concentration and energy for a deceased person to show himself through sight, sound, or kinesthetic means, and the energy lasts only a brief time. If this effort does not coincide with quiet receptivity on the part of the recipient, the visitation will not be registered.

Lamb says a lack of appearance should not be interpreted as a lack of caring. The spirit of our loved one sincerely cares about us and frequently travels back and forth between dimensions to see us. She then makes suggestions for initiating communication, "For anyone who wishes to have contact with someone who has died, it seems helpful to cultivate quiet, private time, focus on the person, and remain in a state of receptivity."

A GLIMPSE OF HEAVEN

Linda was only 44 hours old when she died from a congenital heart defect. Her mother writes from Kentucky to tell this beautiful dream.

After my mother died in September of 1991, I prayed for her to send us a message about our little girl who lives in heaven. Last year she gave me a beautiful gift: a dream of hope and comfort. Let me tell you about it.

In this dream, my parents were walking through a beautiful field of flowers. The colors were very brilliant and luminous. The sky was an intense lustrous blue, the grass was a very bold, downy green that seemed to flow like the waves of an ocean. My parents were much younger, and I could feel their love and joy to be together again. They were holding hands, looking at each other, smiling, murmuring words I couldn't hear, just moving through the field of flowers. Although she never acknowledged my presence, I had the distinct impression my mother knew I was watching.

Then, from a near distance, I heard a little girl's angel-sweet voice call "Grand-Jenny, wait for me!" The voice was joyful and warm and rushing, and I knew right away who it must be . . . our little Linda.

My parents turned towards each other, kneeled down, and looking back the way they had come, held out their arms for her. Mama smiled up at Daddy and said, "Oh, Honey, here comes Linda. She looks so much like Debbie did when she was three years old, except Linda has Paul's dark curly hair. Sometimes, when I look at her, I feel as if Debbie is right here with us, too." And then she smiled so big and radiant her eyes almost shut with joy. "I'm so glad she's here."

I immediately felt a flash of anger: my Mom KNEW how I grieved for our baby! But in the very next instant, I was filled with honor and gratitude that a very real part of me was already spending eternity with my parents. At that moment I seemed to gasp with anticipation that I would soon see Linda, and I quickly pulled away from them, my field of vision instantly becoming narrowed.

The meadow of flowers was in a bright circle of light that gradually, but swiftly, closed. Almost like an eye. That's when I woke up hysterically crying. "I know what Linda looks like . . . I know what Linda looks like!" I felt I had visited heaven for a while and they breathe a different form of air up there. I couldn't quite catch my breath for a moment and Paul was anxious. He wanted to know what his baby looked like, too.

After telling him about the dream, I said, "You know, it's funny. I heard Linda's voice so I know she can talk, and I felt her rushing so I know she can run. And even though I didn't get to see her face, I know what she looks like. And Paul, now I know. She's not a baby anymore. She's growing up in heaven, and someone I love is taking care of her."

That's when I remembered a professional photograph taken when I was about three years old, so in the middle of the night I ran in search of that picture because I knew it would help me "know" Linda. And when I first looked at it, I got one of the biggest shocks of my life!

The date on the back of the picture was the very same as the date on which this dream occurred, thirty four years ago . . . February 1, 1958! When I turned the picture over, suddenly the little girl in that photograph wasn't me anymore, but Linda. Because the very first thing I noticed was the locket she wore around her little neck. The locket was a golden heart. A HEART! The very symbol we use for her since she was born with a congenital heart defect.

It was such an incredible feeling to reach back all those years in time to the circumstances surrounding what must have been the happy day that picture was taken. What happenings had prompted my mother to place that heart locket around my neck all those years ago? And to come full circle to that very day . . . seven years after my father died, five months after my mother died . . . and a grown woman looking at a picture of herself at three years of age. The same age her daughter would be now had she lived. And around her neck . . . a golden locket of a HEART! The dates were incredible, but the heart is what really gave it away. It was all the confirmation I needed. What wondrous, indescribable joy!! I don't have to wonder anymore. Now I know. My baby is THREE!

There are several important aspects of this dream visit. The first is another confirmation that deceased relatives are there for us when we die. The last several dreams have shown us this. The grandfather who takes the child fishing, the aunt who cares for the son, and now the Grandparents who are there for Linda.

The second aspect concerns the scenery in the afterlife. Many people who have "glimpsed" heaven through dream, vision, or near-death experience, tell us the scenery there much surpasses the scenery here. The colors are brighter . . . everything is more vivid . . . the flowers, the trees are more beautiful . . . the sun is brighter. This description comes up again and again in the literature. This dreamer agrees.

The extensive literature about the afterlife tells us that children who die continue to grow in the heavenly realms. They grow to an age in which they are comfortable but never grow old. By comparison, those who die at an old age, never seem to appear old. It is believed they, too, choose an age at which they are most comfortable and appear this way. Remember the grandparents in this dream? They appeared younger . . . and Linda appeared older. She is growing up in the other dimension.

After twenty years of avidly reading books about the afterlife, I have come to believe there is no such thing as coincidence. The Cayce readings tell us that so-called accidents never occur without a cause. Dr. Elizabeth Kubler-Ross, the world famous expert on death and dying, also believes that nothing in life is a coincidence, and all of life's trials have an ultimate purpose. I do not believe Linda's heart locket or the corresponding dates were coincidences.

Dr. Bernie Siegel, M.D. is famous for his work in visualization therapy with those who are dying of cancer. In his best-seller *Love, Medicine, and Miracles*, Siegel states,

> I subscribe to the Jungian idea of synchronicity, or meaningful coincidence. I believe that there are very few accidents. After one of my talks a man handed me a card on which was written, "Coincidence is God's way of remaining anonymous." In a life out of harmony with itself, events seem to conspire to go wrong, but by the same token they mesh wondrously when you start to live your bliss. Don't climb the ladder of success only to find that when you reach the top it is leaning against the wrong wall. As you begin living your life, taking risks to do what you really want to do, you will find things fall into place and you "just happen" to be in the right place at the right time. Even elevator doors start to open when you arrive.

I love the following dream because it has some very important symbolism. This story comes from a mother in North Carolina whose daughter, Karla, died at the age of ten days.

THE TRAIN

Karla was on a train. She was about 18 months old, not 10 days old. But there was no doubt that it was Karla. She was standing there on the end of the car with her blonde hair, waving to me. I knew I had to get to her. I was not frantic. I just knew this wasn't right and I had to get to her. I tried the door closest to her and it was locked. I ran back to the next door . . . locked. And the next . . . locked. When the train started to slowly pull out, I finally got a door open. I had to run to jump on to the train. I was racing through the cars to get to Karla. When I finally got to the car before the one Karla was on, I saw her standing on the platform. She was waving to me and saying, "Hi, Hi Mommy!" Just as I was about to get onto her car, the train separated. Her car went one direction and mine went another. It was a fairly parallel path. I could still see her for a while, waving and smiling.

That was the end of the dream. I woke up and felt very sad, but perhaps less totally devastated than I had been feeling. This dream was about four to six weeks after Karla died.

The mother and daughter are on two separate trains, and the mother cannot get to her daughter because of the locked doors. I believe the locked doors represent the mother's inability to reach the daughter because they are now in different dimensions. This is obviously very frustrating for the mother. The good news, however, is that although they are on separate trains, the trains are on parallel tracks, therefore both going in the same direction. They will both reach their destination, and when they do, they will once again be together in the light.

HUGS

Jessica died in a car accident when she was only 18. Her mother states,

I have had many dreams of her, but I had two dreams that I don't believe were dreams. I felt that I was with her.

Jessica always gave me a hug when she would go out. It started as a joke to get money or stay out later, but then it became a habit. About a week after the funeral, she came to me in a dream and said, "I wouldn't leave without giving you a hug." And then she gave me two hugs. The next morning my other daughter called me and said "Jessica said goodbye to me last night." And later in the day Jessica's best friend called and said the same thing!

About four months later I awoke one morning so happy and peaceful and I knew I had been with Jessica that night. I felt like I had been in a green field with lots of bright sunshine . . . walking and talking and laughing with Jessica. We held hands and walked around together. It was wonderful!

Here again we have a "coincidence." All three people had dream visits on the same night. Did you notice how she spoke of the lovely scenery as did the other mother who had a"glimpse" of heaven?

I'M ALL RIGHT

Sally was killed in an airplane accident at the age of 16. Her mother went to the cemetery and pleaded with her to come and tell her that she was O.K. A few nights later she had this dream . . .

I was in a clearing of trees, surrounded by beautiful flowers and grass, and the sun was shining brightly. Sally walked toward me and motioned that I sit with her on the stone bench that was in the clearing. She smiled and gave me a kiss and a hug, and said, "I'm O.K. Mom, I'm all right." She was wearing a shorts outfit that I had never seen before, and a pair of sandals. I remembered the sandals because Sally had extremely small feet for a young woman that was 5'6" tall. She had the tiniest toes you could have imagined, and I remarked on them. We used to laugh about her small feet all the time. We exchanged no other words and she got up from the bench and walked a short distance away, and looked back at me, and then proceeded to walk a little farther and sort of faded into the setting.

I will remember this dream for the rest of my life!

Although most deceased loved ones appear in clothes that are familiar to us, they occasionally show up in something we never saw before. This dream is very typical since the message states, "I'm O.K," and also because of the beautiful natural surroundings.

Sometimes when a loved one dies suddenly, we are unable to say goodbye or tie up loose ends. The following story tells of how a grieving mother finally finds "closure" after the death of her daughter.

FINDING PEACE

My daughter Jane died from an over-dose of alcohol at age 37. Our last phone conversation before she died was very unpleasant and she was very angry at me. Because of her alcoholism, we had taken care of her two children off and on over the years. She wanted her son to move back with her and I told her I felt he should stay with us one more year and finish his last year of high school. After her death, I had a lot of anger and guilt to work through. After three years I didn't seem to be making much progress until my dream.

I was walking along a street when someone came up to me and said, "Jane is in that house, if you hurry you can see her." I ran into the house and when I saw her we hugged each other and cried. I told her I was sorry and that I loved her. She said, "I forgive you Mom and I love you too."

Upon awakening I felt the peace I had been searching for. I was then able to start the healing process by remembering all the good times we had and the positive things in her life.

Many people who have lost a loved one say they wish they had just five more minutes with them to say goodbye. The people who have had a dream visit are given that gift.

CHAPTER FIVE

VISITATIONS

In the book, *Regression Therapy, A Handbook for Professionals,* Hazel Denning, Ph.D. has the following to say about post-death communication.

> Contact with the dead is quite common. In all probability such visitations would be perceived more often if people were not so frightened of them. If these experiences were not taboo, the reassurance and information they can give could be accepted readily. Following my lectures I have often had individuals share long-kept family secrets about such visitations, incidents that could have comforted family members when they occurred if the significance of these events could have been recognized as a normal part of human relationships.

These returns from former earth residents serve a variety of purposes. Most commonly the entities want to give reassurance that they are all right, that the state of being beyond death is a good one. They come to comfort a grieving friend or relative. Sometimes they return for the purpose of delivering a last message, or they may return periodically to check on former loved ones. At other times they provide information that they feel is of benefit to those left on earth.

Our loved ones come to us in many ways with their message of assurance and love. The following stories are just a sample of the many visitations the bereaved experience.

"Feeling the Presence" is an experience that's hard to explain. Have you ever felt that someone was in the room, even when you didn't hear them actually come in, and then turn around and there they were. Feeling the presence is basically like that, only much stronger. There is NO DOUBT that someone is in the room, only you can't see them. The feeling is OVERWHELMING, and usually will make the hairs on the back of your neck stand up.

A Pennsylvania mother wrote the following story about her husband's communication experience, and shared it in a Compassionate Friend's newsletter.

A FATHER'S DAY GIFT

I am writing this article as a "gift of love" to my husband and our son. I want to share with you a very special experience between father and son. A moment captured in feelings and time from the "otherside."

Last summer we traveled to Seattle for the Annual Compassionate Friends Conference. Before attending the conference, we toured the area, which is so beautiful. We arrived there on Father's Day and drove directly to Mt. Ranier. Our first glimpse of it, from the highway literally took our breath away. It was gorgeous! It was also the FIRST TIME we could see nature and actually see the beauty in this world again since Donald's death.

On Monday, the following day, we were settled in at the lodge and decided to get a better look at the area. This was the day after Father's Day. We stopped at Narada Falls while driving the beautiful back mountain roads. My husband got very quiet as we started down the path to the falls. He was too emotional to speak, and I could tell something overwhelming had happened. He couldn't talk about it until later that day. He said that as we started down the path toward the falls, a great sensation came over him. He felt as if he could have reached out and touched our son. He definitely felt his presence there, at the falls, with a rainbow running through it. That was a moment of "love" between father and son and also hope once again in our lives. It was an experience of great peace for both of us.

About a month after his death, Bobby came to visit his father in a waking vision. His mother tells the story. As the years have passed since his death, his family still occasionally hears his footsteps walking through the house.

A WAKING VISION OF BOBBY

Bobby came to see his dad. Chet woke me up and leaving the bed, said he couldn't sleep and was going downstairs. When I came down to check on him later, I saw he'd been crying and asked him what was wrong. He said Bobby had come to see him, and he was wearing the leather coat we had put in the casket with him. He loved that black motorcycle coat. It was his prize possession. Bobby came through the closed door, and walked between the coffee table and the couch up to where Curt was lying. He never said a word, just touched Curt on his heart the way he had done so many times before when he wanted to show his dad his love for him.

Bobby also came to his sister in a waking vision. On the first Mother's Day after his death, he appeared to her in the draperies of her bedroom. He was smiling and had a glow around his head. He told her, "I'm O.K., and we will all be together again." He smiled and then disappeared.

Many times the vision is only a very short visit, as told in the following stories.

BOUQUET OF FLOWERS

I awoke in the middle of the night, which is very common for me for I usually have to take a "bathroom break" once during the night. I rolled over to get out of bed and there, by my bed, was my sister Mary. Mary had died about two years previously from a lengthy battle with cancer. She was smiling and radiant, but said nothing. She just stood there looking at me. In her hand she held a beautiful bouquet of flowers. As soon as I started to get out of bed, she disappeared. The next morning when I awoke, I remembered it was my birthday. Was Mary giving me a birthday gift?

The medium, George Anderson, often sees the deceased with flowers in their hands. This seems to be a universal symbol of sending love and well wishes.

A VISIT FROM FATHER

I awoke in the middle of the night and at the foot of my bed was my father. He had died many years previously from Leukemia. He just stood there smiling at me, but never said anything. I rolled over to awaken my husband, and when I did, my father disappeared.

On most occasions when bereaved individuals experience a touch, it is when they are in a hypnagogic state. The hypnagogic state is when we are half awake or half asleep, depending on how you want to look at it. It is that moment when we are just waking up or just going to sleep. For some reason when we are in that relaxed state of mind, we are more susceptible to these experiences. I believe when we are asleep, our subconscious mind takes over and our conscious mind rests. When we are half way between both of these states we have the intuition of our subconscious, but can also consciously remember the experience.

In her book, *The Encyclopedia of Dreams*, Rosemary Guiley refers to the hypnagogic state as hypnagogic dreams. She says, "Hypnagogic dreams are those occurring at the onset of sleep, often in the gray "twilight" between consciousness and unconsciousness." She goes on to explain how this type of dream is similar to the experiences of meditation or psychedelic drug use. One may hear someone whispering or calling their name or have a feeling of floating or falling. She says that although these hypnagogic experiences are mostly verbal, they can also be visual, consisting of lights or colors which may "develop into simple geometric patterns or sometimes complex designs." Although I have always used the term hypnagogic for waking up and falling asleep, Guiley defines hypnagogic as when we are falling asleep and "hypnopompic" as when we are awaking.

A MOTHER'S DAY HUG

This Illinois Mother received a blessed gift from her deceased daughter on Mother's Day. She writes:

It was Mother's Day, and we had been gone all day visiting my Mother about an hour away in another state. I was feeling quite bad about missing Sara on the day I was meant to spend with ALL of my children. I was quite exhausted, and fell into bed. I don't remember dreaming at all except I woke up still feeling Sara's embrace around my shoulders. It was so vivid to me that it felt like she had held me all night long. I heard her whisper, "Happy Mother's Day." At first I felt that I was a little crazy, and that it was only a dream, but I really felt her there! It was one of the best experiences of my life other than the day I delivered her into this world.

KISSES ON THE COUCH

A widow from Wisconsin writes:

My husband died after a ten month battle against cancer. He was only 58 and his death has left a piece of my heart misplaced. I was fortunate to have him home the last 3 1/2 weeks of his life and I was right by his side when he left me. I was happy to be able to devote myself to his needs, and we promised each other at that time that we would try and communicate in some way after his death . . . AND WE HAVE!

Several months after his death on a day when I was having a very hard cry, I felt his hands cup my face and gently kiss my cheeks. My eyes were closed at the time and my head was lying back on the sofa. The experience made me suddenly sit up in shock, but it was a pleasant shock.

The following unusual physical happenings were experienced by a grieving family in Missouri after the death of their son, Bobby. The stories are told by the mother.

THE ROSE

We placed a "closed" red rose in the casket, and as the family was standing around the casket the rose opened. We believed it showed us that his love was with us.

OPEN THE GATE

It was close to Halloween, my son's favorite time of year. I wanted to get him a pumpkin for his grave because nothing else was there except the funeral flowers and the metal marker the funeral home puts at the grave site. My step son drove me to the cemetery to put the pumpkin on Bobby's grave. When we arrived at the cemetery car entrance, one of the gates was closed and one was open and we couldn't get through. Before we could get out of the car to open the gate, it opened by itself. We looked at each other and immediately knew Bobby had opened it. Not a breeze was blowing or a leaf moving.

A CHANGE IN THE BEDROOM

It was Christmas and my daughter and I had just arrived home from placing a Christmas tree on Bobby's grave. We went into Bobby's locked room because his "smell" seemed to linger there. The shotgun shell holder that Bobby had made was not hanging on the gun rack where it belonged but was lying on the bed. I wondered why my husband had put it there, but when I asked him about it, he said he hadn't been in the room for weeks. We looked at each other and immediately knew that, once again, Bobby was showing us his love was as great as ours.

THE SIGN

After Christmas, I began to worry if Bobby was happy where he was and I asked my step daughter to pray for me to have a "sign" that Bobby was happy. Several days later, my husband and I had been out late and when we came home we walked through the dining room with the lights out. I bumped into a chair that should not have been in my path. When we turned on the light, we saw that the chair from the opposite side of the table had been moved. We believe the only reason the chair was there was because Bobby was telling us he was happy in heaven. God does answer prayer and allows the deceased to give us signs to ease our pain. This was my turning point. Bobby was happy!

The mother concludes, I really feel he helped all of us through this terrible time. I feel it all happened from God's great love for us. After all, He was a parent too. There was a reason for his sudden death. I don't know why, but I know there has been a definite change in all of our lives. Our marriage became much stronger as we faced this together. God's love is so great. I wish everyone could feel that love as we have been able to. I still have "blue" days all these years later. The "missing" is still with me, especially when I see a young man his age, now with a young family. My belief is what keeps me going. I love you, my beautiful son, and I always will.

THE CHRISTMAS GLOBES

A grieving mother from New Jersey states, There have been a few times when I am reading or just sitting in the living room when one of my Christmas water globes will just start playing and Santa will start to go around. I guess it is just Sonny's way of letting me know he is here with me.

THE INCREDIBLE JOURNEY

The spring after Donald died, our daughter, Lisa, and her husband walked for M.S. Lisa carried several blue foil heart-shaped balloons. It was a rainy day and after the walk was completed, only one balloon had some helium left. Lisa and Charlie were married and lived with us at the time. Their bedroom was down on the first floor of our 2-story home. Lisa put the balloons in their room that night.

The next morning I went to the second floor and looked into Donald's room. The balloon was sitting in the middle of the arrangement we had at his funeral which sat at the bottom of his bed.

Charlie was sitting at the kitchen table and I went down to thank him for placing the balloon there. When I did, he said, "Is that what happened to it?", and told me neither he nor Lisa had put it there. I also asked my husband, but he didn't place it there either. Apparently that balloon, with very little helium in it, and no air current through the house, made its way upstairs with no help from any of us.

It came out of Lisa's room to the kitchen, under an archway, turned right under another archway, and into the dining room. From the dining room, it made a sharp right turn and went up our flight of stairs to the second floor. At the top of the stairs, it could have gone left to our room or right to the bathroom, but instead it made another sharp right turn into Donald's room and landed exactly in the middle of the funeral arrangement. This is how it had to have happened, we checked all other possibilities.

My question until this day is, did our son carry the balloon, or was an angel sent to show us he was O.K.?

A SIGN IN AN APPLE

It was the morning of my little son's baptism. Although a baptism is a joyous and happy day, it was overshadowed by the fact that one member of the family would not be there. My brother, Mark, had died several years before at the age of 22. I was particularly thinking of Mark today because my son, Jared Mark, had been named after my deceased brother.

I went to the market early to do some last minute shopping for our family celebration. My family has always teased me about my shopping habits when buying fruit. I always stand there and inspect and feel every piece of fruit, making sure that it is perfect before I decide to buy it. This was a special day, so I was very particular about the beautiful red apples I bought.

Unknown to me, that morning my sister, Jenny, had made a special request to my brother, Mark. She asked him to give her a sign that he was there with us on that special day.

When I was getting the fruit out of the refrigerator to prepare our table, I was overwhelmed when I looked at one of the apples. Carved deeply into it was a sign of the cross! Mark, in his own way, had shown us that he, too, was at our family celebration. Jenny was given the sign she had asked for!

AN EASTER GIFT

My seventeen year old son was killed in a car accident two weeks after Easter. At Easter time he had given me a gorgeous gardenia plant which I kept in my living room. When he died, so did the plant. I kept it in the living room for a while until it looked too bad, and then I carried it to the basement because I did not have the heart to get rid of it. The basement was dark and I never watered the plant.

A year later, on the Thursday before Easter, I went to church to take communion. I was at such a low ebb, the depression seemed to envelope me so completely that I did not want to live.

When my husband and I got home from church, I could not sleep, so I got up and went to the basement to do some laundry. When I walked into the basement, I saw that the dead gardenia plant had three beautiful blooms on it! I ran upstairs to call my husband, and we could not believe our eyes! By Easter morning, there were six blooms on it, and then the blooms died and I was able to finally get rid of the plant.

Why did this dead plant come to life again? Could this be a supernatural happening? I believe so.

HELP FROM A KITTEN

About a month after my son, Bill, was killed, I was in his room and was asking him to give me a "sign" that he was all right. As I was puttering around, his kitten, Moo Shu (named after his favorite Chinese food, Moo-Shu pork, because the kitten was found behind a Chinese restaurant), jumped on his desk and knocked over a glass painted bottle. I freaked out because I didn't want anything touched in his room. As I went to pick up the bottle, I put my index finger into the neck of it and found something inside. I started pulling it out, but it was tightly rolled up inside. I tried putting it back, but it became wrinkled, so I pulled it all the way out. It was a piece of paper written on in magic marker by my son. It simply said, "I love you, Mom." I couldn't believe it! If Moo-Shu hadn't knocked the bottle over, I would have never found my message.

A DAUGHTER'S PERFUME

A mother from Minnesota wrote me a brief note stating both she and her husband were awakened from a sound sleep when the odor of her deceased daughter's perfume permeated their bedroom. She was waiting for a dream visit in which she could speak with her child, and was disappointed that she had only received an odor as a message. No one knows why these experiences are sent in different forms for different people, but I believe they are messages none the less. Why does one spirit come in a dream and another send a smell? I wish I knew the answer.

In chapter one, I explained how many visions of the bereaved are precognitive and how in some unexplained way, the deceased or a member of his family have a premonition of the upcoming date. People in the organization MADD (Mother's Against Drunk Drivers) have discovered that many people who are killed by a drunk driver have some kind of premonition before the actual event. Teens may write poems about their own deaths in the weeks before a fatal accident. As you know from chapter three, my son Andy did exactly that.

Carl Jung, the famous philosopher and psychiatrist, believes we can catch glimpses of the future through the Collective Unconscious. He believes the future is unconsciously prepared long in advance and that is why many of us receive premonitions of it.

Edgar Cacye taught that anything which happens on the physical plane is dreamed about before it actually happens. According to Cayce, the subconscious mind can envision the future, and time in the subconscious realm is not the same as in the realm of consciousness. The idea of the future is alien to the subconscious because it just sees things a they are presently headed. Cayce personally began having warning dreams about the 1929 stock market crash two years before in 1927!

In his book, *Love, Medicine, and Miracles*, Bernie Siegel, M.D. states how he has encountered many cases of precognition when working with his patients. He believes there are "hidden channels of communication from the unconscious to our conscious minds." Siegel states:

> Time after time in my experiences with patients I encounter unconscious knowledge of the future. One Monday I operated on a man named Mike, who had a massive hemorrhage from an aneurysm that had ruptured into his esophagus. It was impossible to stop the bleeding, and he died. When I talked to his wife, she said, "You know, Sunday we spent the whole day discussing his funeral and will , and I said, "Why do we have to talk about all this morbid business? and now I know."
>
> Several times I've found that close relatives knew of a person's death before they had received news of it. My own father, who is now almost eighty, told me a few years ago that his mother visited him—spiritually—one day at work when he was a young man. She said goodbye. He knew she had died, and he grew terribly sad. His coworkers noticed, but he couldn't tell what had happened because it sounded crazy. As soon as he got home, the phone rang, and his sister told him their mother had died.

Mark Thurston, *Dreams, Tonight's Answers for Tomorrow's Questions*, explains that even though subconscious minds can contact one another, the information must first pass through the subconscious mind of the recipient and may be distorted by his own fears or thoughts. This is why not all precognitions are accurate. Thurston explains how the future is not permanently fixed into the subconscious. He says, "Since the future is not fixed, no psychic or precognitive dream can say for certain that something specific will happen. However, it is possible to be sensitive to what will happen IF things follow their current pathway."

Elsie Sechrist, in her book *Death Does Not Part Us*, tells us that everything that happens in our world is the result of happenings in the spiritual realms of existence, and we can "experience them as we would shadows cast by coming events." Sechrist tells us how psychics are able to see these "shadows" before they happen in the physical world; and, through dreams, many of us can pick up on these thought forms.

The views of Betty Eadie, *Embraced By The Light*, parallel those previously mentioned. While having an extended NDE, Eadie was shown how everything is created in spirit before it is manifested in matter. She says that "spirit creation could be compared to one of our photographic prints; the spirit creation would be like a sharp, brilliant print, and the earth would be like its dark negative. This earth is only a shadow of the beauty and glory of its spirit creation."

A mother from Ohio wrote to me about her 23 year old son who was killed on his motorcycle. The son, Derrick, does not appear to his mother in a dream, but to a friend, who, in turn, calls the mother and relays the message. I'm not sure why this happens. I believe some of us are more susceptible to dream visits than others, and if the deceased is having difficulty communicating with one person, he may try another. This dream also gives a premonition.

A MESSAGE FROM DERRICK

Derrick had a lady friend who we did not know. The Christmas after his death she called me and said she had had a very real dream about Derrick. In the dream, Derrick said to her, "Sherry, please call my Mom and let her know I am fine. She is so distressed over me." Sherry said they talked about different things and then Derrick said he had to go because a friend of his Dad was going to die. Sherry said, "Derrick wait! Who is it?," but he was already gone.

A week later I was reading our newspaper and told my husband, "Can you believe this? Brad's dad died and he was only 52! Brad was a school friend of Derrick." Then I remembered the dream!

This mother continues, "I am a Christian and have a strong belief in Heaven. But you know how depressed we become just struggling to keep our heads above water . . . how we miss our child beyond belief, and even though we believe, we long for confirmations that they are O.K. I believe God gives us or others dreams of our child to help us to know He is taking care of them."

This same family experienced another precognitive dream. The mother writes:

About two weeks before my father died of a sudden heart attack, Derrick's girlfriend told me she had dreamed that "Papa" had a heart attack. She said that in the dream he was going upward and was very happy. Because my father didn't have a heart condition that we knew of,

I never mentioned it to anyone. When I called her to tell her about the sudden death she said, "Remember the dream?"

A MEMORABLE HOLIDAY

This story comes from a Compassionate Friends newsletter.

I am not writing here to sadden anyone, but as a tribute to LOVE, FAMILY, AND FAITH. On December 6, 1985, my daughter, Mary, was murdered. While gathering her things to bring home, we found Mary had lovingly made Christmas gifts for everyone in the family. Family came from Florida, Canada, Arizona, and here in Georgia and remained through the holidays.

Sometime before the incident, my daughter told me that she had a dream that the whole family was together at Christmas time and she was outside the window looking in. She said that in her dream she felt such a feeling of contentment at seeing us all together. It had been years since all of the family had been together.

We decided to have Christmas as Mary would have wanted it. My husband and I wrapped the gifts Mary had so lovingly made for those she loved. On Christmas morning, while we were opening the gifts, my husband told me to look out the window. There are two rocking chairs on the porch and one was rocking back and forth. My husband reached over and held my hand, and it was at that moment I remembered what Mary had told us about her dream, and I realized then that her dream had become a reality.

Mary was still with all of us and was indeed content at watching the family she loved so much sharing the joys of Christmas together.

I also realized Mary would always be watching me and that, though in one sense she had been taken from us, she would always be a part of all of us. The little gifts she made for everyone that Christmas would be treasured for many Christmases to come, but what would be treasured most was her LOVE OF FAMILY and the FAITH of knowing that one day we will be together again.

A friend of my family's told me this story about a precognitive dream:

EXPERIENCING IT TWICE

In 1948, when I was in my twenties, no one ever spoke of anything like ESP or psychic phenomena. One night I had a vivid dream about my friend from church, David. David had just come home from the service, and we were all glad to see him once more.

In the dream, I was at David's funeral. Our minister was presiding over the service and I saw David lying in his coffin surrounded by beautiful flowers.

I sang in the church choir with David's sister, Marion, and I told her about my dream. When I did, she said that her grandmother had just been speaking about a strange feeling she had about something bad happening to David. Marion was going to be married in several weeks, and David said to her, "If anything would ever happen to me, I don't want you to postpone your wedding."

Several days after my dream, we received a phone call telling us that David had drowned while swimming in the local river. When I went to the funeral, it was an exact repeat of my dream. I watched our minister offer the service, and saw David lying in his coffin.

After the funeral, I spoke to my minister about my precognitive dream, and he told me I must be close to God for him to reveal that to me. At first I was worried that maybe I should have done something to prevent this tragedy, but I eventually realized there was nothing I could have done.

In a previous chapter, I spoke about the fact that we all have a time to die. This was obviously David's time.

THE FLAT-BED TRUCK

A Pennsylvania mother writes this story of her precognitive dream:

Right after Donald died, I hoped I would dream of him. I missed him so badly. The one dream I finally had surprised even me. I never had a dream that told me ahead of time what would happen.

Donald had a Cordova car which was sitting off to the side of the driveway. Weeks after he died, we finally decided to sell it. He also had a little V.W. Rabbit which we kept and still drive. The Cordova was too big and we just couldn't keep the two cars. We advertised it in the paper and we had a family come out to look at it. They started it up, looked it over, and decided to take it. They didn't come for it right away because we had papers to take care of at the Notary.

A few weeks before all of this took place and before we put the car up for sale, I had a wonderful dream. In my dream the Cordova was sitting on a flat-bed tow truck in our driveway. Inside the car sat our son, Donald. He was handsome and looking the same age as when he died. He had a smile from ear to ear, sitting behind the wheel of the car. I tried to go get my husband (in my dream) but at that point I woke up. I had to cry, but I also had a great sense of peace that Donald was O.K.

When the folks came for the car, it gave them problems and wouldn't start. So they said they'd be back with a tow truck. I figured the regular tow truck would come to get it. I was completely dumb-founded when a flat-bed roll-back truck came to pick up the Cordova. When he loaded it up, it sat there exactly as in my dream weeks before. I took pictures of it, I just couldn't believe it! Although I couldn't see Donald (as I had in my dream), I was sure he was there and he was smil-ing . . . "it's O.K., Mom, and so am I."

BIRDS AND BUTTERFLIES

According to Carl Jung, throughout the history of man there have been certain basic recurring patterns of images, symbols, and themes which he labeled "archetypes." Jung believed these archetypes came from the great pool of knowledge which he called the "Collective Unconscious." This knowledge is available to all men through their subconscious mind. Through my extensive research on the visions of the bereaved, I have come to believe the bird and the butterfly are two archetypes which symbolize the eternal nature of man. The ancient Egyptians used a butterfly to symbolize life after death.

Candy Lightner, *Giving Sorrow Words*, states that birds are a mythological symbol of the soul, and presents the following story of a widow: "After my first husband died, I felt his spirit continually for a period of a few weeks. Every time I would come to the parking lot where I worked and walk from my car to the office, I saw the same bird. And it sang to me and would follow me. And I thought that very definitely was his spirit."

As I mentioned in chapter two, Elisabeth Kubler-Ross, the world-famous expert on death and dying, found that when she did art therapy with children who were dying, they often drew pictures of cocoons and butterflies. This, of course, symbolizes that although the cocoon looks dead, the butterfly emerges and is free to fly away. These children, even if they were not told they were going to die, somehow realized they would soon be a beautiful butterfly. When allied soldiers occupied Nazi concentration camps, they found pictures of butterflies drawn all over the walls of the children's dormitories.

In his book *Love, Medicine and Miracles*, Bernie Siegel, M.D. tells the following story,

Paula, one of our ECaP group members, told me of an experience after her daughter was murdered in a brutal assault at her college. At the murder's trial, a bird appeared in the window, making an awful racket and disturbing the proceedings. Paula said she knew it was her daughter, because she always demanded a lot of attention. Later at the wedding of Paula's other daughter, another bird appeared, cackling raucously, interrupting the outdoor ceremony. Then after Paula finished telling this story in the group, a bird began squawking at the window, and everyone turned to Paula and said, "I guess that's your daughter again."

Then Siegel relays his own personal story:

> Recently I was out jogging on a cold, dark December morning. A bird followed me for half an hour, chirping and sharing with me. When I came home, I said to Bobbie, "Someone died and just said good-bye." Wednesday I got a phone call and learned that a patient I'd been very close to, who was in another state, had died at that time.

A Pennsylvania mother writes about her experience with a butterfly in the form of a poem:

DONALD'S BUTTERFLY

When I finally found you, I wondered what color would you be and how you would look?

I searched high and low on vacation. I saw many of your new friends, but I didn't see or feel your presence.

Then one blue and very down day, there you were. While visiting friends for a picnic (I wasn't much in the mood). As I was walking up their lane in a field of clover and wild carrots, there was a beautiful yellow and black butterfly.

I had my camera so I started to photograph. This butterfly left me get very close and did not move very far from me. I photographed from many angles, as if it were posing for me.

Then I looked down upon its wings and wondered: Might I be able to touch this beautiful creature? Twice I stroked between its velvety wings. It fluttered but never moved. Then I knew it was Donald's presence . . . "DONALD'S BUTTERFLY."

BUTTERFLIES ON A TAPE

I found this story in a Compassionate Friend's Newsletter:

When Robbie died in June of 1989, age 26, we had his apartment to empty. Among his things were many audio tapes he had bought over the years. My other son and daughter took the ones they wanted and I also took a few. I put all these tapes into our stereo cabinet and that's where they stayed until March of 1993.

I took a train trip to Memphis in March of 1993 and decided to bring tapes to listen to on the train. I took one of Robbie's and a Bob Sieger tape. (I didn't use them on the train)

Four days after arriving, my friend Charlene and I went to a beautiful little lake. I was laying on a pier thinking about the beauty that surrounded me. My thoughts turned to Robbie and how sad it was that he would never see such beauty on this earth ever again. I decided to listen to some music and I took out his tape. The original wrapper was gone and he had written who made the tape and folded the paper like the original cover would have been.

I put the tape in and began to listen to his music, really getting in touch with how much I missed him and how I wished he was here on this beautiful lake. As I sat there, I took the tape case and removed the piece of paper he had written on. I unfolded it and turned it over. The only thing on the other side of that piece of paper was two butterflies. To me it was a message that he was fine, and not to feel sad because he was with me always.

I've often wondered why I took that tape after not touching it for 4 1/2 years. Why that moment when he was so much in my mind did I choose to take it all apart; to find that little gift, that message he had for me. I guess "why" isn't important. Some things aren't to be questioned, but are sent to us as gifts from our beloved children.

THE RELEVATION

In April of 1978 my beloved son Tim was killed in a senseless drunk driving accident. On this day, time seemed to stand still as if it were frozen in time and space. Where he had gone? I wondered. Is he in heaven or what has happened to him? I was tormented and needed to know for certain that he had gone to heaven. The torment and the raw bitter pain of losing him and the thought that I would never see him again in this life was more than I thought I could bare.

Tim was killed 2 weeks after Easter. A week after he was buried, my husband, daughter, and I visited his grave. We were on our way home in a rainstorm, a real downpour. My daughter was driving and I was sitting up front. Suddenly, a butterfly swooped down in front of the windshield on my side. I said, "Did you see that?" But neither of them had seen it. I felt a quickening of my heart and I knew it meant something, but I wasn't sure what.

A few days later we went to church and I looked up at the cross that was placed in the church for Easter. Before Easter, this cross was bare, and now it was filled with beautiful artificial butterflies. Then the Relevation came to me. "That's it! Tim is ALIVE, and he now has a beautiful body just like a butterfly. Since that time I have had numerous butterfly happenings.

It was Tim's birthday and I woke up offering a prayer there would be a sign that he knew I was wishing him a happy birthday. I had a butterfly chime hanging in the bedroom, but the air was still and the chimes were not moving. Suddenly my husband said, "Look up at the ceiling." Across the ceiling were butterfly lights going back and forth and back and forth. I was astonished. In a few seconds they just raced across the wall like they were "going crazy." I said from my heart, "Tim, you tricky little devil you! Happy Birthday!"

When my husband died, four years after my son, Tim, my brother and his wife invited me to their cabin in the mountains for a weekend. I had taken my knitting with me and had been knitting on the porch, when I laid it on their picnic table to go inside with my sister-in-law.

After a while, my brother came in and said, "You must come out here and see how this butterfly sits on your knitting." We all went out and watched for quite sometime as it just sat there. I finally picked it up and started knitting again, but the butterfly kept trying to sit back on it. The butterfly was still around the next day. Was this a sign that all was well with my husband?

A mid-west Compassionate Friends group held a special meeting to remember their deceased children. They went into an open field each carrying a helium balloon and let them go together symbolizing the love they sent toward the heavens. The balloons all flowed upward together and then miraculously formed into the shape of a butterfly!

In the book, *Regression Therapy*, Barbara Lamb, M.S. explains how the deceased may bring us messages through physical means; not only by moving objects but by "visiting in the form of a live bird or animal who carries the distinct sense of the presence of the person." Lamb believes, as do I, that these visits are actually from spirit. Our deceased loved ones come to us for a variety of reasons.

Lamb states:

> They seem to want to be seen, heard, recognized, and accepted for who they are. They want to reassure us about their continuance after death and give us hope about ours. They seem eager to let us know that the love relationship and caring continue, even after death. They want to complete unfinished business. They want to be remembered. They want to help us, guide us.

CHAPTER SEVEN

SOURCES OF INFORMATION ABOUT THE AFTERLIFE

If you would ask the average American if he believed in an afterlife, he would say yes. A Gallup poll taken in the 1980's showed that seventy percent of the American public believe in life after death. If, however, you asked him to describe what the afterlife is like, he wouldn't even venture a guess. Christian religious texts are very vague about the afterlife. Most of what we visualize about heaven comes from early European paintings of angels among the clouds. If asked what one does in heaven, he might say, "I don't know, sit on a cloud and play a harp?"

How could anyone possibly know about life after death? There are, surprisingly, many sources of information. History provides many ancient documents about the afterlife. Millions have experienced near death. Psychologists who practice regression therapy have patients who describe an afterlife filled with beauty and wisdom. In all times in history, man has written about psychics and visionaries who seem to be able to 'know" things the general public does not, and many of them have told us about their "glimpses" into the beyond.

As we have discovered in the past chapters, those who visit us from beyond the grave also give us clues to what life is like on the other side. In dream visits, we sometimes catch a glimpse of beautiful scenery. We also become aware that those who have died have the same personality as they did when we knew them in life. The deceased tell us what they are doing or how they are watching over us, and always seem to be aware of what is happening in the physical world. Death bed visions are a common occurrence, and the visions of the dying tell us those who have gone before still have a loving connection to us because they "come to get us" when we die. Those who are dying also describe loving angels who surround them, brilliant white lights, colorful flowers, green pastures, crystal clear streams, and gorgeous sunsets. Amazingly, all these sources reveal stories which are strikingly similar.

If we have so much evidence about the afterlife, why doesn't anyone know about it? The answer, of course is the same as why no one knows about the visions of the bereaved. It is not taught in schools, and many who have such experiences don't talk about them because they don't want to be thought of as "crazy." You never hear anyone at a cocktail party sitting around discussing life after death. Most of us don't know there have also been many books written about the afterlife, and the information in them is basically the same. I have 65 such books in my own library.

As I now present some of these experiences, theories, and stories, you, too, will have an opportunity to see how they parallel.

SOURCES FROM HISTORY

Plato

Plato, one of the greatest philosophers in history, lived in Greece from 428 to 348 B.C. Unknown to many of us, however, Plato had interesting beliefs concerning the spiritual nature of man. Raymond Moody, in his book *Life After Life*, explains how the theories of Plato parallel the near-death experience:

> Plato believed strongly in the use of reason, logic, and argument in the attainment of truth and wisdom, but only up to a point, for in addition he was a great visionary who suggested that ultimately truth can only come to one in an almost mystical experience of enlightenment and insight. He accepted that there were planes and dimensions of reality other than the sensible, physical world and he believed that the physical realm could be understood only by reference to these other, 'higher" planes of reality. Accordingly, he was interested in the fate of the soul after physical death and several of his dialogues—especially *Phaedo, Gorgias*, and *The Republic*—deal in part with that very topic.

According to Moody, Plato's work often describes death in a way that is strikingly similar to the near-death experience. Plato defined death as the separation of the soul from the physical body, and believed our spiritual body is far less limited than our physical one. He also believed that time, in the other realms of existence, is not the same as time in the physical world. Time in the physical is only the "moving unreal reflection of eternity."

Just as in the near-death experience, Plato explains how, when we die, we will once again be able to visit with others who have also passed away. Moody says,

> In various passages, Plato discusses how the soul which has been separated from its body, may meet and converse with the

departed spirits of others and be guided through the transition from physical life to the next realm by guardian spirits. He mentions how some might expect to be met at the time of their death, by a boat which takes them across a body of water to "the other shore" of their after-death existence.

Plato explains how our physical body is the "prison of the soul," and states we exist in spirit before we enter the physical world. Moody explains:

> According to Plato, the soul comes into the physical body from a higher and more divine realm of being. For him it is birth which is the sleeping and the forgetting, since the soul, in being born into the body, goes from a state of great awareness to a much less conscious one and in the meantime forgets the truths it knew while in its previous out-of-body state. Death, by implication, is an awakening and remembering. Plato remarks that the soul that has been separated from the body upon death can think and reason even more clearly than before, and that it can recognize things in their true nature far more readily. Furthermore, soon after death it faces a "judgment" in which a divine being displays before the soul all the things . . . both good and bad . . . which it has done in its life and makes the soul face them.

As was explained in chapter two, many near-deathers tell us how they had the opportunity to review their lives, both good and bad, and how they were NOT judged by the "Being of Light," but were supported and loved as they judged themselves. Moody explains how, in Plato's "Republic," Er, a Greek soldier who was near death in a battle, journeyed into the other realms of existence:

> First of all, Er said, his soul went out of his body, he joined with a group of other spirits, and they went to a place where there were "openings" or "passageways" apparently leading from earth into the realms of the afterlife. Here the other souls were stopped and judged by divine beings, who could see at a glance, in some sort of display, all the things that the soul had done while in its earthly life. Er, however, was not judged. Instead, the beings told him that he must go back to inform men in the physical world concerning what the other world was like. After seeing many other sights, Er was sent back, but he said that he was ignorant of how he was returned to his physi-

cal body. He merely woke up and found himself upon the funeral pyre.

Plato explains how, when we are in our physical bodies, we are limited to our five senses which, in some ways can give us the wrong impression of things. Our souls cannot see true reality until they are free from physical distractions.

The Tibetan Book of the Dead

The Tibetan Book of the Dead is taken from the ancient wisdom of Tibetan lamas. It is basically a book of instructions for the dead and dying, the original text having been written in the eighth century A.D.

In order to keep the dying person's consciousness focused in the right direction, sacred names and prayers are repeated to him. This parallels the last rites of the Catholic church. The ritual is designed to create the correct consciousness while entering the afterlife, or the Bardo.

In the first stage after death, the spirit consciousness is in a trance-like sleep, unaware it has left the physical body. At this time, the spirit is aware of the Clear Light, but is unable to recognize it. At the end of the first Bardo, the spirit realizes he has died, and then slips into another sleep and "dies" into the next level or Bardo. When he wakes up in this Bardo, he sees visions or thought forms which are based upon his own personality. He believes he possesses a body like the one he had on earth, but this is only an illusion. In fact, everything in this second Bardo is an illusion. Those who are truly enlightened, pass this Bardo and go directly into paradise.

How we think on the earth plane effects what happens to us in the Bardo. "As men think, so are they, both here and hereafter, thoughts being things, the parents of all actions, good and bad alike; and, as the sowing has been so will the harvest be." In the second Bardo one's thoughts could create a hell for the evil doer. According to the Tibetan lamas, the visions seen in this Bardo are not real, but hallucinations and thought forms of one's own consciousness. It is almost like a dream state in which the dead becomes a spectator of hallucinatory movies. The goal of the deceased is to surpass this level of illusions and reach Nirvana, or oneness with God.

In the second Bardo, the god, Dharma-Raja, is the judge of the dead. As other deities look on, he weighs one's black pebbles (bad deeds) on one side of the balance scales against his white pebbles (good deeds) on the other. Devils wait to lead the evil doers into the hell world.

If the deceased does not slip into the Clear Light of Nirvana, he goes into the third Bardo where he prepares to reincarnate into another physical form.

The Egyptian Book of the Dead

The original papyrus of the *Egyptian Book of the Dead* was written somewhere between 1500 and 1350 B.C. It is not one book, but actually a collection of funerary texts which were written by ancient Egyptian priests who composed them for the dead. It includes spells, hymns, litanies, magical words, and prayers.

From ancient times, the Egyptians believed in eternal life and the resurrection of the spirit-body. These beliefs are based upon the legend of Osiris, who after experiencing a cruel death, was resurrected. Osiris was the Lord of Creation who became the King of Egypt. He and his wife, Isis, ruled Egypt well, but Set (the evil one) murdered Osiris. Osiris then became the King of the afterlife and rose again in his new spirit body. Other names for Osiris are the "King of Eternity," "King of Kings," and "Lord of Lords." Osiris represented the destiny of every human, and the Egyptian's identification with him reminds us of the Christian identification with Jesus Christ. According to the Egyptian Book of the Dead, when we go to the afterworld we will become the "Son of God" and eat from the tree of life.

The doctrine of eternal life is the major feature of the Egyptian religion. All religious worshipers hoped to have a new life in the "Other World." It was not the physical body which would rise again, but the soul, or spirit body. The preservation of the physical body was essential, however, to ensure the eternal life of the spirit. The spirit body lasted forever and could ascend into heaven and dwell with the gods and the souls of other righteous men.

To the Egyptians, man did not consist merely of a spirit body and a physical body, for the system of belief surrounding the body was a complicated one. Man was believed to consist of a physical body, a spirit body, a heart, a double, a heart-soul, a shadow, a spirit-soul, and a name. All parts were bound together to form one whole.

Upon death, man dwells, eats, and drinks with the gods, wearing the white robes they wear. He is never again hungry or thirsty. When speaking of heaven, some texts tell us it is divided into seven halls or mansions, all of which the spirit had to pass through in order to eventually be with God. The soul journeyed from one heavenly district to another, traveling toward his meeting with Osiris. The soul was called BA and was represented by a hawk with a human head.

According the "Book of Gates," life in the "Tuat", or Other World, was pleasant for those who were protected by Osiris, but those who were not, lived in darkness and misery. The Egyptians, however, did not believe in purgatory or everlasting punishment. Those who were wicked were burned in the fire, but this was only a one-time happening; the punishment did not go on forever.

Funeral ceremonies varied from dynasty to dynasty. A funeral ceremony from the 5th and 6th dynasty tells how the god Osiris will accept the burden of the dead man's sins, and how the dead will be purified by a sprinkling of water. There were many varied funeral rites to assist the dead in his journey through the Other World.

Just as in the Tibetan book of the dead, there is a judgment. Instead of pebbles being weighed on a scale, however, the deceased's heart is weighed against an ostrich feather, the symbol of truth. The spirit's guardian angel accompanies him to this judgment. If one's heart is found "true and right" he is allowed to enter into the presence of Osiris. Truth, honesty, and harmlessness were a few of the virtues needed to pass the judgment. The god Osiris hated "lying, prevarication, deceit, and insincerity." After he passes the judgment, the soul joins the other truthful spirit souls who will live eternally with the god Osiris.

The Egyptian Book of the Dead is lengthy and complicated, and varied from one dynasty to the next. The preceding review is only a sampling of the whole in order to give you a general idea of the beliefs of the ancient Egyptians.

THE NEAR DEATH EXPERIENCE

In recent years several books have been written by individuals who have had extended near-death experiences in which they were shown various aspects of the life after death. As you read these stories, you will discover how the basic information given by each person has many common characteristics.

George Ritchie, M.D.

George Ritchie, M.D. "died" in 1943 in a military hospital after a respiratory illness. He woke up late at night, got out of bed, and not finding his uniform in his room, went out into the hall in search of it. As he passed someone in the hall, they walked right through him, and when he found himself outside of the hospital, he was floating approximately 500 feet above the ground! All Ritchie could think about was how he had missed his train to Richmond, so he began to speed eastward watching forests and rivers pass below him as he headed toward his destination. When he "landed" in a small town and met another person who walked right through him, Ritchie began to believe he must be dead. The thought of being dead at 20 frightened him, so he turned around and began to speed back to the hospital to find his body so he could once again occupy it.

He quickly returned to the hospital, searching all of the rooms for his own body, but had difficulty finding it. He finally identified "himself" by his fraternity ring which was on his finger. No matter how hard he tried, he couldn't re-occupy his body. As he began to feel lost and discouraged, the light on his bed began to grow and brighten until it was a blinding, radiant white. Something inside of him said "Stand up, you are in the presence of the Son of God."

As a "Magnificent Being" came out of the light, the hospital walls dropped away and Ritchie saw a panorama of his entire life flashing before him. This "life review" is a documented common aspect of an NDE. Ritchie explains how there are no words to adequately describe what he saw and experienced. This Being of Light, whom Ritchie believes was Jesus, made him feel more loved and accepted than anyone on earth ever had. Ritchie was not judged during his life review but was loved and supported as he watched his good and bad deeds pass before him.

He and the Being of Light communicated through their minds, not through their mouths. When the life review was completed, Ritchie understood that it was not his "accomplishments" or physical wealth that was important in the review of his life, but the giving of LOVE. When Ritchie stated he was too young to die, the Being of Light answered, "No one is too young to die, for physical death is only of the body and a temporary doorway to another realm through which you have passed."

Ritchie was then shown five realms of existence in the afterworld, which he describes.

1. *The Physical Realm*
In this realm of existence those who have died remain in the physical world because of their attachment to it. Ritchie was shown spirits of those who were alcoholics who did not pass into the light but who "haunted" bars, trying to get another drink.

2. *The Astral Realm*
The astral world was in another dimension but seemed to be somehow intermingled with the earthly world. This realm was less dense and material than the physical world, although much like it, and was divided into separate levels of existence. One's level of existence seemed to correspond to his way of thinking. Those who thought the same way seemed to be somehow linked together. Some of these levels were loving and good, others were not, as it all depended upon how you thought. In this level, Ritchie saw hospitals which he labeled "receiving

stations" that were there to help people adjust to this new realm of existence. He also stated some people arrived in the afterworld in a deep hypnotic-type sleep.

3. *Hell*
Hell was filled with hate, deceit, lies, self-righteousness, and sexual aggressiveness. This was not a hot, fiery place, but a place that was void of love. Although it was destitute, angels hovered around it waiting for anyone to ask for assistance. This was not an eternal state, but was self-chosen; and when someone wanted out, all they had to do was ask for help, and the angels would help them with their spiritual growth.

4. *Realm of Knowledge or Paradise*
Learning, knowledge, hope, and joy were the key words for this realm of existence. There were great learning centers where one could study anything which was of interest to him. Those on this level of existence understood that LOVE was the most important aspect of our being, and one's race, color, or creed, was of no importance.

5. *The Celestial Realm*
To reach this realm, Ritchie traveled away from the earth, for it was not intermingled with the physical world as were the others. This heaven was filled with beings of light and overwhelming love.

After his "tour" of the afterworld, Ritchie was led back into his room, but he clung to the Being of Light, unwilling to leave it. The next thing he knew he was waking up in his hospital bed. Ritchie tells of his experience and how it profoundly changed his life in the book *My Life After Dying*.

Betty Eadie
Betty Eadie was hospitalized in 1973 for a hysterectomy. While recuperating, she experienced what has been called the "most profound NDE ever." In her book, *Embraced By The Light*, Eadie recounts the truths she learned, the people she met, and a description of the spirit world which she entered.

At the beginning of the experience, Eadie felt a surge of energy and then was drawn upward with a feeling of freedom. As she hovered above the hospital bed, she realized the body lying there was her own. As she floated near the ceiling, she remembered thinking "this is who I really am." Three men suddenly appeared at her side and introduced themselves as having known her for "eternities." Through images in her mind, she began seeing herself in her existence before her physical life as well as her previous relationship with these three men. Eadie states, "The fact of a pre-earth life crystallized in my mind, and I saw that death was actually a "rebirth" into a greater life of understanding and knowledge that stretched forward and backward through time."

As many others who have had similar experiences, Eadie explains how communication was not verbal. She says, "They communicated much more rapidly and completely in a manner they referred to as "pure knowledge." She not only "felt" what they were saying, but also felt their emotions. As Dr. Ritchie, she found she could pass through the hospital walls and saw trees rushing below her as she began to speed toward home. When she arrived, she saw her husband and family. Although she felt their love, she felt a stronger desire to move on.

As she heard a rushing sound, she fell into a vast blackness and began to move at an incredible speed. This was not frightening, however, but gave her a feeling of complete tranquillity. The blackness began to form into the shape of a tunnel with a small pinpoint of light at the end. At the end of this tunnel, she was greeted by a being who was bathed in a brilliant white light. This being exuded complete love and Eadie felt as though she had come home. She believed this figure to be Jesus Christ and she knew she had known him before because she actually remembered him. The being said, "Your death was premature, it is not yet your time."

Eadie explains how, at this time, many questions were answered for her. The answers came as quickly as she could think of them. She learned earth is not where our spirits originated, but is only a temporary school. In this school, we learn to abide by the laws of creation and learn that love is supreme. Our individual talents are gifts to be used in service to others in love. No matter our religion, color, or physical appearance, each of our individual spirits are filled with love, light, and eternal energy.

According to Eadie, when we meet someone we don't like, it is because they have qualities which remind us of something within ourselves we need to change. Hate, envy, and unforgiveness destroy the spirit. She says, "I understood the perfection of the plan. I saw that we all volunteered for our positions and stations in the world, and that each of us is receiving more help than we know. I saw the unconditional love of God, beyond any earthly love, radiating from him to all his children. I saw the angels standing near us, waiting to assist us, rejoicing in our accomplishments and joys."

Eadie learned there are two major energy forces in the universe . . . negative and positive. As spirits of energy, we have the free will to use either of these energies to create our own reality. We on earth do not yet understand the power of our own thoughts. The spirit controls the mind and the mind controls the body. Through our thoughts, we can ward off illness or create healing. It is our own thoughts which draw either positive or negative energies to us.

While in the physical world, our spirit chooses experiences for our own inner growth. This may be illness or accident, but any experience is an opportunity for learning and progress. Eadie explains, "We are here to learn, to experiment, to make mistakes. We don't need to judge ourselves harshly; we just need to take life one step at a time, not worrying about other people's judgment of us, nor measuring ourselves by their measuring sticks. We need to forgive ourselves and be grateful for the things that help us grow. Our most severe challenges will one day reveal themselves to be our greatest teachers."

Next, Eadie met two deceased friends who gave her a guided tour of the afterlife. She was shown places where people were working together on projects of mutual interest. These were spiritual projects which would eventually manifest in the physical world. She was also shown a library void of books. The knowledge you desire would be transferred directly into your mind.

Eadie was shown a beautiful garden where all things worked harmoniously for the glory of God. While there, she not only felt at one with everything in the universe but realized all of us are ONE. As did Ritchie, Eadie was shown the afterlife as having many levels of development and that our spirit will automatically go to the level in which it is most comfortable. She was also guided through other worlds and galaxies and was shown we are not God's only creation.

Eadie met spirits who were preparing for their descent into matter. Those spirits who are "friends" in the spirit world come to earth as family and friends. She explains how this is a "spiritual bonding" due to an eternity of being together in love. As does Helen Wambach, Eadie tells us we choose the circumstances of our own lives, our parents, our strengths, weaknesses, and purposes. We also choose the time of our own "death" before we ever enter into the physical world. When a child dies, it was part of its divine plan to do so and although there is grief for the parents, when we are united again in the light all pain is washed away. According to Eadie, "Coming to earth is much like selecting a college and choosing a course of study."

As we go through our earthly existence, there are angels who come to guide us along the way. We will only be guided, not forced, because we need to make our own choices through our free will. The most important thing in life is the love and service we give to others.

As she experienced a life review in front of a counsel of men, her life "flashed" before her. The counsel did not judge her, but lovingly supported her in this experience. As she did this, she came to realize that none of us actually make mistakes, but only have experiences for inner growth. Forgiveness is very important, and we must first forgive ourselves before we are able to forgive others.

After the review, she was told she must return, which she did not want to do. When she was shown her life's purpose, however, she agreed to come back. Eadie tells us how her glimpse of eternity taught her that EVERY soul has infinite worth. We are all watched over by a multitude of heavenly angels. She explains, "We are all equal in their eyes, great or small, talented or handicapped, leaders or followers, saints or sinners. We are all precious and carefully watched over. Their love never fails us."

Dannion Brinkley

In 1975, Dannion Brinkley was hit by a bolt of lightning that came in through his telephone line. What happened after that is quite amazing. He saw his own body lying across the bed as a feeling of peace and tranquillity came over him, and he watched from above as his wife tried to revive him and the ambulance rushed him to the hospital.

A tunnel began to form in front of him and he willingly went through it, as he was drawn to the light at the end. As he came into a brilliant white light, he saw a Being of Light that radiated a deep sense of love. Brinkley then experienced a life review in which he watched his life, good and bad deeds, pass before him while the Being of Light looked on in nonjudgmental compassion. This Being of Light did not communicate with him verbally but with some kind of mental telepathy. The Being said, "Humans are powerful spiritual beings meant to create good on earth. This good isn't usually accomplished in bold actions, but in singular acts of kindness between people. It's the little things that count, because they are more spontaneous and show who you truly are."

After flying over majestic mountains, Brinkley found himself in what he describes as a city of crystal cathedrals. There, in a center for learning, thirteen Beings of Light gave him premonitions of events yet to come in the world. Of the 117 revelations, 95 have already occurred. He was told the premonitions were not "cast in stone," but could be changed by man because, although he did not realize it, man was a great spiritual being who can co-create with God.

Brinkley was informed he must return to earth in order to create centers which would help people reduce stress and come to the realization who they really were . . . spiritual beings. When we realize we are spirit, our fear subsides and we become more loving to our fellow man.

He then found himself floating in the corridor of the hospital and realized the body on a guerney covered with a sheet was his own. As he once again occupied his body, he felt the fire and pain which was the result of his injuries. Realizing he couldn't move, he blew on the sheet which covered his face to let those who were about to wheel him into the morgue know that he was indeed alive. The surprised orderly rushed him to the emergency room instead of the morgue.

During his long convalescence, he kept trying to tell everyone about his experience, but no one really wanted to listen. Then something happened which changed his life . . . he saw an article about Dr. Raymond Moody and the near-death experience. Moody was going to give a presentation at a near-by college. After he met Moody at the presentation, he was granted a personal interview that developed into a lasting friendship. From then on, he began to fight desperately to get well because he now knew he wasn't crazy and that his life held a definite purpose.

Brinkley eventually began to help Dr. Moody and started to go on tours with him. As time went on, Brinkley began to realize he had developed psychic abilities. He began to answer people's questions before they asked them. When he looked at people, he sometimes could see visions about what was happening in their life. When he touched an object, he could see visions of the owner. He explains how, as he toured with Moody, he learned that many others who had had NDE's also developed unusual psychic abilities.

Other visions also appeared to him. He was shown information concerning the healing centers he was to create. He says:

> Through the visions I began to realize certain things about the human body, one of which being that, like these transducers, we transmit spiritual, mental, and physical essences of ourselves to the world around us. By learning to be in touch with our electrical and biological selves, we can make ourselves higher beings who transmit the spiritual side of life.
>
> My visions about the centers were all about understanding the body . . . how it produces energy and how that energy can be found in such a way that it has a spiritual context to it. When you reach the point where you can control this energy and transform it into a positive force, you have found the part of you that is God.

Thirteen years after the initial NDE, Dannion developed pneumonia and a staph infection which lodged in his lightning-damaged heart. He needed immediate surgery, but would not sign the consent form because he felt as though he was ready to die and had absolutely no fear of doing so. Raymond Moody was the one who finally convinced him to have the needed surgery.

While in surgery, Dannion "died" once more and was met by the same Being of Light. He experienced a second life review. During this review he was told he must forgive all those who had ever done wrong to him, because if he didn't, he could not go upward to the next "spiritual level." He then began to move upward with the Being of Light. He explains:

> We moved upward through dense fields of energy that changed color from dark blue to a whitish blue, at which point we stopped. Then the Being's pitch lowered and we moved forward. Again, as in the first experience, we flew toward a range of majestic mountains, where we dipped down and landed on a plateau.

He was then shown a greenhouse with beautiful flowers and an environment of complete relaxation. He was told, "This is the feeling you are supposed to create in the centers." After he was told he must once again return, he was suddenly back in his body.

Although Brinkley was not given a tour of heaven as was Ritchie or Eadie, he was shown how all of us are spiritual beings who, when we leave the physical body, have a spiritual one. We still have the same thoughts and feeling we had in our physical body and can be aware of what is still going on in the physical world. Death does not have to be feared, and through his hospice work, Brinkley learned how many dying patients are visited by those in spirit. This experience brings about feelings of love, joy and peace. He explains how he is secure in the knowledge "there is a spiritual system that takes you from this world to the next."

REGRESSION THERAPISTS

Another wealth of information about life after death comes from psychologists and psychiatrists who practice past-life regression. Although many American psychologists scoff at this procedure, thousands of highly educated and credentialed mental-health specialists find this procedure very beneficial to their patients. When in a relaxed or hypnotic state, the patient can be regressed back to, not only his own birth, but before, into the time preceding his incarnation into this world. These patients tell us about their experiences in the other realms of existence.

I can hear many of you saying, "But I am a Christian, and I don't believe in reincarnation. Therefore, anything written about this is not a valid resource for me." Believe it or not, some psychologists who practice past-life regression do not believe in reincarnation. How can that be? There are several theories about where these memories come from. The first, of course is they come from past lives. Another theory is that of Jung's Collective Unconscious and how this pool of knowledge stores the memory of all that has ever been. Although psychics are able to "dip" into this pool for information, when in a hypnotic state or when we are dreaming, most of mankind also has access to this knowledge. It is a feasible answer to ESP. Edgar Cayce, America's most famous psychic, also speaks of a great pool of knowledge and memories, which he calls the Akashic Records. Some believe that when we experience a past life, we are actually experiencing someone else's life as it is stored in the Collective Unconscious. Some experts have theorized that the memories of our ancestors are somehow carried to us in our DNA. Who knows? These are, however, theories which somehow may give an alternative explanation to the theory of past lives.

In her book *Embraced By The Light*, Betty Eadie tells how, while having a near-death experience, she was shown information about our genetic coding and how our memories from our spiritual existence are contained in the cells of our physical bodies. She explains:

> I learned that all thoughts and experiences in our lives are recorded in our subconscious minds. They are also recorded in our cells, so that, not only is each cell imprinted with a genetic coding, it is also imprinted with every experience we have ever had. Further, I understood that these memories are passed down through the genetic coding to our children. These memories then account for many of the passed on traits in families, such as addictive tendencies, fears, strengths, and so on. I also learned that we do not have repeated lives on this earth; when we seem to "remember" a past life, we are actually recalling memories contained in the cells.

Many Americans seem to be knowledgeable about their own particular religion, but know little else about other religions. We go to church every week to learn what our particular denomination says, but are never introduced to the teachings of other religions. I believe every student in high school should take a course in comparative religions, so they can compare their belief system to those of others. When I studied comparative religions, I was amazed to find how similar the basic ideas of each religion are.

For most of us, the word reincarnation conjures up visions of an Eastern Yogi draped in white linen and sitting on a bed of nails. Most of us do not know that the theory of reincarnation is also part of some

Western religions. An early Christian sect known as the Gnostics taught the theory of reincarnation up until the Council of Nicia around 325 A.D. At this time Emperor Constantine made Christianity the official state religion and deleted all references to reincarnation from the New Testament. As seemed to be the practice of the time, he then proceeded to eliminate all other sects who did not agree with his beliefs. The only thing left of the Gnostics are some of their writings. Other early Christians who believed in reincarnation were Clement of Alexandria, Origen, and Saint Jerome. An esoteric branch of Judaism that studies the Kabbalah also holds a belief of reincarnation, as do many Native American tribes. If anyone you know tells you that reincarnation is strictly an Eastern belief, they have not done their homework.

Helen Wambach, Ph.D.

Helen Wambach, Ph.D. completed a study in the 1970's in which she traveled all over the country hypnotizing various groups of people with varied backgrounds. Through hypnosis, she regressed her subjects to the time of birth, and then beyond to the time right before. The results of this study, reported in her book *Life Before Life*, give amazing insights to questions not only about the life after death, but the nature of our existence in general.

Of the 750 subjects who reported a birth experience, 81 percent relayed to Dr. Wambach that they remembered choosing to be born. Although the final choice seems to be up to the individual spirit, many of the subjects reported consulting with some kind of advisor or group of advisors about the decision of being born into physical life. Many of them felt that incarnation was some kind of service or duty and they were basically reluctant to come into the physical world. Only 28 percent of the subjects who remembered their pre-birth existence actually felt enthusiastic about being born.

When speaking of those who counseled them before birth, the subjects made no distinction between people who were alive at that time and people who were dead. When in the spiritual existence before incarnation, whether a person was physically alive or dead seemed relatively unimportant. There also seemed to be a different kind of time system, and the element of time seemed to have little importance in this spiritual state before birth.

It is interesting to note that seventy percent of the people hypnotized mentioned they chose to be born into this time period because it was going to be a time of great development in spiritual awareness for mankind. They described how we would become aware of our "oneness" and realize we are linked together on higher planes of existence.

Many said the latter part of the twentieth century would also have earth changes and social upheavals.

According to the survey, most subjects believed their true "inner self" was neither male or female, but chose which sex it wanted to be in the upcoming life. They also stated they had not only incarnated to have experiences, but to learn lessons from these experiences. The general consensus was that one could learn to lead and "demonstrate mastery" as a male, but it was easier to learn lessons and show love as a female.

When asked why they chose to be born at all, most subjects answered they came here to learn to love without being possessive or demanding. Twenty-eight percent, however, stated their life's purpose was teaching mankind "to understand his unity with others and to develop his higher consciousness." This higher consciousness is a knowledge how we are all linked together as part of "one giant soul organism." We are one, not only with other humans, but also with God.

Most subjects stated they had had many previous lifetimes, and the important people in this life were also people they had known in past lives. The relationships were not confined to past lives, however, but continued into the other realms of existence. Wambach states, "We come back with the same souls, but in different relationships. We live again not only with those we love, but with those we hate and fear. Only when we feel only compassion and affection are we freed from the need to live over and over with the same spirits, who are also forced to live with us!"

Although the subjects of the study were a mix of various religions, all subjects were unanimous on one key point. When asked when the soul entered the fetus, they stated the fetus was not part of their consciousness. They were a fully conscious entity and not a part of the fetus until around six months of gestation; and then they were only "in and out" of their body. (This is very similar to how Elisabeth Kubler-Ross and the authors of *Final Gifts* tell us those who are dying go in and out of their body) Although not always in the fetal body, the subjects were all telepathically aware of their mother's emotions.

Thirty-three percent of those interviewed stated they never joined the fetus at all until just before, or during birth. The subjects also stated how their soul can elect to leave the fetus or the infant body at any time they choose. Wambach suggests that according to this study perhaps Sudden Infant Death Syndrome may be a result of a soul's decision not to enter physical life at this time.

When asked about the birth experience itself, sixteen percent of those interviewed stated they never experienced birth, but entered the body after it was born. Of the eighty-four percent who actually remembered a birth experience, most of them stated birth was a sorrowful process and being in a body was not only very confining after a life in spirit, but also that it was difficult to leave the beautiful "land of light," which one experiences in the other realms of existence.

Dr. Wambach concludes that many people will not like the results of her study and she will probably be accused of influencing her subjects. This, however, is not the case. All she did was ask the questions, not suggest any answers. As you will see, other psychologists who have used hypnosis in order to find out about the life beyond have been given basically the same answers.

Brian Weiss, M.D.

Dr. Brian Weiss, M.D. is a graduate of Columbia University and Yale Medical School and is the Chairman of Psychiatry at Mt. Sinai Medical Center in Miami. As a traditional psychotherapist, Dr. Weiss was astonished when, under hypnosis, one of his patients began to recall a past life. His original skepticism began to fade, however, when this patient began to deliver messages about Dr. Weiss's deceased father and son.

The patient, who Weiss names Catherine, came to him for treatment of anxiety and panic attacks, which at some point he decided to treat with hypnosis. According to the doctor, hypnosis is actually only a state of focused concentration and is an excellent tool for helping a patient recall forgotten incidents. When she was under hypnosis, Dr. Weiss told Catherine to "go back to the time from which your symptoms arise." To his astonishment, Catherine began to talk about a previous life in 1863 B.C.! He didn't know what to think. The patient was not delusional nor was she Schizophrenic. Where were these memories coming from?

As time passed, Catherine spoke of other life times, and as she began to recall them, not only did the problems of anxiety and panic attacks begin to disappear, but she began to develop psychic abilities. Sometime during hypnosis, Catherine would know what questions Dr. Weiss was going to ask before he asked them.

During one session, Catherine described her own death and spoke of seeing a bright white light. While remembering what it felt like to be "dead" she told Dr. Weiss, "Our task is to learn, to become God-like through knowledge." It seems that while Catherine was in the afterlife existence, she could converse with those she called "Masters" who explained universal laws and knowledge to her.

Every time Catherine would experience the death of a past life, she would float above her body and then be drawn into the bright energizing light. Many times others would come to greet her, welcoming her into the light. During one session, Catherine stated she had information about Dr. Weiss's deceased father and son and spoke of how each of them died. This was knowledge she did not consciously possess.

Catherine told him her "Masters" had given her this knowledge. Dr. Weiss reveals that this event irreversibly altered the course of his life. According to Dr. Weiss, the knowledge of life and death he received from Catherine helped him to be a calmer, happier, more patient person. He believes Catherine was able to tap into her "superconscious" mind while under hypnosis and also believes each and every one of us could also have this ability if we chose to work on it.

According to Catherine, there are many levels and dimensions in the world beyond, each one having a higher level of consciousness. What plane we enter upon death depends on our soul's progression at the time.

Catherine eventually became completely cured of her anxieties and panic attacks, and Dr. Weiss continues to use past-life regression successfully with other patients. Dr. Weiss says,

> I do not have a scientific explanation for what happened. There is far too much about the human mind that is beyond our comprehension. Perhaps, under hypnosis, Catherine was able to focus in on part of her subconscious mind that stored actual past-life memories, or perhaps she had tapped into what the psychoanalyst Carl Jung termed the collective unconscious, the energy source that surrounds us and contains the memories of the entire human race."

Dr. Weiss believes the universal knowledge he gained through Catherine has changed his life forever and has given him a basic understanding of life and death and how this universe functions. In order to obtain more information about Dr. Weiss's experience, you can read his book entitled, *Many Lives, Many Masters*.

Joel Whitton, M.D., Ph.D.

In his book *Life Between Life*, Joel Whitton, M.D. explains how some of his patients who were regressed by hypnosis spoke of their existence in the afterlife. According to his research, the soul leaves the body upon death and enters a timeless and spaceless state. Dr. Whitton begins by explaining how only four to ten percent of the population are able to enter a trance which is deep enough to actually experience this mode of existence. Once in the interlife, the patient reaches a higher level of awareness which goes "far beyond our earthbound conception of reality." He labels this extraordinary state of perception "meta-consciousness."

The ancient Tibetans called the existence after death the "Bardo." According to the author, when one is in the Bardo, he feels at one with the universe and yet while feeling this oneness with everything, somehow feels more self-aware than ever. Most people find it very difficult to explain this realm of existence in words and in order to "translate" the experience, draw subconsciously on universal symbols (Jung's arche-types) from the Collective Unconscious. The patient who is able to symbolize the experience, can explain his feelings while the one who can't is relatively uncommunicative. One subject saw his name in a book in the form of a symbol, but when he tried to verbalize it, he could not. This essential telepathic mind communication seems to be how one "speaks" in the afterlife.

According to Dr. Whitton, while in the Bardo, the patient feels re-laxed, peaceful, and filled with wonder, and somehow comes to an un-derstanding of how he has chosen the circumstances of his earthly life. Time, however, is not linear as in the physical world. The author says, "From the earthbound perspective, there is no logic; there is no order; there is no progression—everything is happening at once!"

Just as those who have explained a near-death experience, Dr. Whitton's patients had the standard "tunnel experience" and then came into the light and were greeted by either a Being of Light, a deceased relative, or some kind of guide. They also had the standard life review, and many of them appeared before a wise counsel of three, who lovingly assisted them with the review of their life but never made any judgments.

Some of those who experienced the interlife described great halls of learning where they studied all manner of subjects. Many of them, how-ever, had difficulty explaining what exactly they had studied because they were unable to put what they saw into a conscious vocabulary.

Just as the patients of Helen Wambach, these individuals spoke of planning an upcoming life while yet in spirit. Dr. Whitton explains how when the spirit enters into the physical body, all memory of the life be-tween life is erased because it passes through "an etheric barrier which serves to lower the vibrations of consciousness."

Through his experience with hypnosis, Dr. Whitton has come to be-lieve that man's nature is basically spiritual and when the soul leaves the body at the moment of death, it returns to its "natural home" and to an awakening consciousness of extreme understanding and clarity. All pa-tients who have experienced the interlife tell of how it is not only a home-coming, but an eventual preparation for the soul's next incarnation into physical existence. And they all clearly stated how our individual soul has many incarnations into the physical realm.

Dr. Whitton explains,

> The next world, being our natural home, brings awakening and remembrance and the restoration of clarity. And in seeing ourselves as we truly are, we are able to learn from the last ex-

pedition into earthly reality, assess our progress, and eventually plan the next incarnation according to our needs."

Winafred Blake Lucas, Ph.D.

In her two-volume masterpiece entitled *Regression Therapy, A Handbook for Professionals*, Winafred Blake Lucas, Ph.D. presents mini-treatises in various areas of altered state work by the leading experts in the field. In one chapter entitled "Varieties of Interlife Experience," Lucas presents the experiences of other doctors and psychologists in relation to the life after death. She explains how memories of the interlife received under hypnosis facilitate a transformation of consciousness just as does the NDE. Unlike the NDE, however, the afterlife which is experienced through regression can be studied more thoroughly because it is chosen and controlled.

When a patient has a joyful interlife experience, his attitude about death forever changes and all fear falls away. When one experiences a life review under these circumstances, they seem to be able to understand mistakes they have made and are more willing to make changes for the better. Lucas explains how this "cosmic consciousness" state of awareness experienced when one is in the interlife can be obtained not only through an NDE and hypnosis, but also through "profound states" of meditation, some psychedelic experiences, and the holotropic breathing techniques of Stanislav Grof.

While in the interlife, effective therapeutic intervention can be made as the patient tries to correct old destructive patterns and change them for the better. It is especially helpful for those with a history of anger, violence, and self-centeredness because, while in the interlife, they are offered a greater insight into their behavior.

In this same chapter, Roger Woolger, Ph.D. explains how many of his patients who experience "death" while under hypnosis have the same basic aspects of an NDE. They float above the body, feel a sense of peacefulness, see a bright light, and are greeted by friends, guides, or a "robed figure in white who radiates love and wisdom." They also meet a "committee" who helps them to review their life. Many see beautiful scenery such as celestial gardens, mountains, and islands. When explaining how these experiences resemble an NDE, Dr. Woolger states, "The apparent resemblances persuade me personally that these are archetypal or universal experiences of death and transition that are recorded in the collective unconscious of the individual."

PSYCHICS

Throughout history, people who had visions have been revered for their special abilities. From ancient Egypt into the modern day, every culture had men or women who could "see things" others could not. In primitive cultures, these people would become the shaman or medicine man. In other cultures, they became special advisors to the king, or maybe a high priestess. During the dark ages, when Europe was drowned in poverty, ignorance, and superstition, the Catholic Church had the sole right to judge if these people of vision were saints or witches . . . whether they would be canonized, or burned at the stake. The fear of witchcraft and those with special gifts continues in some Christian denominations today, as they continue to label anyone with psychic ability to be "of the Devil," even when these people continue to do good deeds for others and lead lives of service.

In the past fifty years or so, our modern culture has been so "science bitten" we have ignored the abilities of such people, calling these special gifts impossible. In recent years, however, there seems to be a shift in thinking. More and more television specials are presenting encounters with angels, cases of ESP, and stories about people with psychic abilities. Many police departments now use psychics to assist them in difficult cases. As the turn of the century approaches, I hope we can look forward to an extending acceptance of those with unusual or psychic gifts.

Many times, those with psychic abilities are privileged to glimpse the afterlife. I will present the theories and experiences of several of America's most well-know psychics.

Edgar Cayce

Edgar Cayce is America's most well-known psychic. As I presented in chapter two, he did thousands of trance "readings" in which he successfully diagnosed both illnesses and cures of thousands of people. All of his work is documented and filed at The Association of Research and Enlightenment in Virginia Beach.

In the book *Death Does Not Part Us*, Elsie Sechrist presents a collection of various experiences with post-death communication and a review of what the Cayce material has to say about the life after death. She says, "Each human being is a portion of God, created by Him and out of him. So there is within each of us that imperishable part that is divine. Being divine, this part of us can never die. It may lie unconscious or asleep within us for a long time—as we measure time—but it can never be lost or destroyed."

Within the mind of each of us is a divine element . . . a consciousness which is part of God. This spiritual aspect within ourselves is what passes over into the other realms of existence at death. Cayce refers to death as entering "God's other chamber." Death is only a change in consciousness and through this consciousness, we are able to better experience our relationship with God. The only thing which has died is the physical body. Sechrist describes death as "a step in the soul's journey back to its Creator."

According to the Cayce material, our deceased loved one continues to be aware of what is happening on earth. We know this by the thousands of cases of post-death communication. They will come to us to tell of upcoming events, or to offer support and guidance with our day-to-day problems, whether they be personal, financial, or health related. They might just drop in to say "Happy Mother's Day!"

Cayce tells us that sometimes, when we die slowly, the spirit is able to communicate with those on the other side and then come back again. This is in complete agreement with what the two hospice nurses tell us in *Final Gifts*. After working with thousands of dying patients, Elisabeth Kubler-Ross relates the exact same phenomenon.

Upon death, we slip into a higher dimension of consciousness . . . a dimension beyond time and space . . . where we experience an expanded level of awareness. Cayce calls this the fourth dimension. In this dimension, all is thought, and although everything is made up of thought forms, this world is vivid and real.

Elsie Sechrist tells us our after-death experiences depend on what we have created for ourselves. She says, "There is no single after-death experience that will be met by everyone. Through our individual actions, we ourselves build our own heaven or our own hell. What we choose to do with our lives, through the exercise of our God-given will, determines the condition we will pass into at death." Cayce said that 'mind is the builder," not only in the physical realm, but in the beyond. Our inner thoughts and our intents mold our lives both here and there.

Sechrist presents what she terms the "phases of spiritual development" which one experiences in the afterlife:

1. A period of unconsciousness and/or disorientation.
2. A time of healing and awakening.
3. An interval of activity as a spirit still close to the earth plane.
4. A period of existence in non-earthly dimensions.

When the soul leaves the body, it is automatically attracted to the spiritual environment most suited to it. This will be a state of consciousness which best suits the soul's growth. Each soul will progress and develop further. As our soul develops, it goes on and on into higher dimensions.

When we pass on to the other realms of existence, our personality remains basically the same. We have the same likes, dislikes, attitudes, and beliefs. In reading 254-92, Cayce says, " . . . do not consider for a moment . . . that an individual soul-entity passing from an earth plane as a Catholic, a Methodist, an Episcopalian, is something else because he is dead! He's only a dead Episcopalian, Catholic or Methodist."

As do those who have had an NDE, Cayce explains how most of us enjoy a happy life in the other realms of existence in beautiful surroundings and peaceful love.

Mary T. Browne

Mary T. Browne is a renowned psychic who is famous throughout the world. Since the age of seven, she has been able to see into the other realms of existence and communicate with those on the other side. In her book, *Life After Death*, Browne describes the world we live in after physical death.

Brown explains that passing over is much like what those who had an NDE tell us. The silver cord which connects our soul body to our physical body does not break in an NDE, however, She tells how those who are dying will begin to see spirits of the deceased who are coming to greet them into the other world. As does Elisabeth Kubler-Ross, she explains how many of the dying are thought to be having hallucinations. Of course they are not. They are just beginning to make the transition. After the transition is made, they will experience a life review.

Upon arrival, many souls need to rest, for it takes a great deal of energy to "die." How long one sleeps or rests depends upon his spiritual understanding. Those who are truly enlightened pass over quite easily. Nonbelievers, however, need time to rest and acclimate.

According to Browne, the afterlife is divided into various realms, and as we grow spiritually, we go higher and higher into the upper levels. She says,

> There are many different realms in devachan. We earn our place through our spiritual development and character. It's like climbing a ladder. Each rung brings us closer to the top. Some climb slowly and with fear, others quickly and fearlessly. Eventually, everyone arrives at the peak. The process is the key.
>
> When we arrive and are greeted by our loved ones, we will notice how everything is more brilliant and vivid than on

earth. The colors are breathtaking. The landscapes and gardens are exotic and lush. Activities in the afterlife are greatly varied and we will automatically be drawn to the activity which interests us the most. If you choose to study, instructions will be made available. There are great libraries and halls of learning. You may live in a lovely home if you so desire. Browne explains, "You reside in the place that you have earned. Those who deserve peace will not be disrupted. As each of us has different ideas of happiness, we are given many choices."

According to Browne, we maintain our own personality and individuality. When we are in the physical life, we work on our own character, but when in heaven, we are allowed to rest and "recharge." As our spiritual nature grows, we become more and more peaceful.

Browne has been shown the hell-like levels of the other dimensions. This hell is only for the most "depraved, remorseless, and evil people," however. Those in hell have damned themselves into this dark region, but are given many chances for redemption. Those who do not repent can live there indefinitely. She explains, "Even the tiniest glimmer of remorse frees a soul from this self-damnation."

The world of spirit is a world of thought, and we can create what we want when we want it. Everything is composed of thought forms. Although this world is not composed of physical matter, all we create within our thoughts is absolutely real. If you want to go somewhere, you simply focus your mind on where you want to be and you are instantly there. Thoughts are just as important in the physical life as they are in heaven. We build our own reality by the way we think. While you are in the physical, you are building thought forms which will go with you into the afterlife. Browne reminds us of Proverbs 23; verse 7, "As a man thinketh in his heart, so is he."

We can prepare for our own death by releasing anger and negativity. Focus on the good things in life. Be thankful, forgiving and especially loving. Try to be of service to others whenever you can. Browne ends her book by saying, "Death is rebirth into the life of the spirit."

Emanuel Swedenborg

Emanuel Swedenborg (1688-1772) lived in eighteenth century Europe during what is known as the Age of Reason. This era in history is well known for its advancements in science, government, and philosophy. Born in Stockholm, Sweden, he was the son of a Lutheran Bishop who taught at a theological seminary. Swedenborg was well educated at university and his major interests were math, mechanics, astronomy, chemistry, and music. His genius is plainly shown in his drawings for a mechanical carriage, a flying carriage, and a vessel to travel under the sea.

After graduation from college, he traveled extensively throughout Europe and then came back to Sweden where he became a member of the Swedish congress. He eventually was employed by the King of Sweden as an assessor of the board of mines. Throughout his lifetime, Swedenborg published many scientific and philosophical works, but by mid-life he was devoting most of his efforts to philosophy.

According to his diaries, Swedenborg's "spiritual sight" began to open in 1743 and gradually developed over a two-year period until he was able to, not only see and hear the other realms of existence, but converse with those who dwelled therein. He spent the remainder of his life publishing philosophical works and recording his spiritual experiences in his diaries.

Swedenborg wrote a lengthy description of life "beyond the veil." He tells how he had the pleasure of conversing with many friends he knew who had died. According to his writings, those who are dying are attended to by angels and those loved ones who are already in spirit. Once the spirit arrives in the other dimensions, he automatically associates with others who are of the same spiritual natures. Once he finds the level most suited to him, he lives a similar quality of life as he experienced on earth. This other world is so much like this one that many refuse to believe they have actually died. This world, however, is bathed in a brilliant light. Our spiritual body is as real as our physical one, and we still have all five of our senses. Our thinking abilities, however, are more acute even though we carry with us our thoughts, beliefs, and prejudices from our physical life. We remain either male or female and most of us appear to be the age of early adulthood. He states, "Man loses nothing by death, but is still a man in all respects although more perfect than when in the body."

According to Swedenborg, there is a judgment in heaven, but man is his own judge and, as his life passes before him, he sees all the good and the bad he has done and learns from it. There is a hell, but no one is SENT there. Those with wicked thoughts seem to naturally gravitate to a place with those of like mind, and remain there until they desire to leave. There is no such thing as divine punishment. There is, however, divine order and law in all aspects of eternity. He tells us there is an equilibrium in all things and evil punishes itself. He says,

> The Lord never sends any one into hell, but is desirous to bring all out of hell; still less does he induce torment; but since the evil spirit rushes into it himself, the Lord turns all punishment and torment to some good and use.

He explains how there is mercy even in punishment.

> The mercy of the Lord involves all and everything done by the
> Lord towards mankind, who are in such a state that the Lord
> pities them, each one according to his state; thus He pities him
> whom He permits to be punished, and him also to whom He
> grants the enjoyment of good. It is of mercy that He permits
> man to be punished, because mercy turns all the evil of punish-
> ment into good.

According to Swedenborg, there are many levels or subdivisions in
the heavens, and one gravitates to his correct place through divine order. If you strongly desire to see someone, all you have to do is think
about them and you will instantaneously be by their side! Life there is
full of busy activity, because useful service is what brings one into heavenly happiness. People work at whatever interests them at the time . . .
art, music, government, science, literature, helping the less fortunate.
The landscapes and architecture of the other world far surpass anything
in the physical, and all of this beauty is created by pure thought.
Swedenborg's works have been published by the Swedenborg Foundation and entail over twenty volumes which extensively explain in detail
all aspects of the life after death.

George Anderson

George Anderson is one of America's most well-known contemporary psychics. Three books have been written about his life and works:
We Don't Die, We Are Not Forgotten, and *Our Children Forever.* Anderson has proven his extraordinary gifts not only through thousands of
readings, but also by submitting himself to dozens of scientific tests.
The accuracy of his psychic communications with the dead is uncanny.

George grew up in a suburban Long Island Roman Catholic family.
After a life-threatening case of chicken pox at the age of six, George
began to see and hear those in other dimensions. As a child, George
could not only tell people what happened to them in the past, but what
was going to happen to them in the future. Because of the negative re-
actions of others to his special abilities, George learned to keep silent
about his psychic gifts. On occasion, however, his visions would be so
overwhelming, he could not keep himself from telling his classmates.
This often resulted in punishment from the nuns at his Catholic school.

By the time George reached high school, his parents and teachers
were dismissing his visions as fantasies, and as a result of his psychic
abilities, he was almost completely ostracized by the other students. His
visions finally became so intense, he confided in some of the nuns. This

resulted in George being sent to a psychiatrist who prescribed such a high dose of Valium that George not only was constantly sleepy, but his brain was so numbed he stopped having visions. Eventually, however, George was sent to one of the state psychiatric facilities. The psychiatrist there could find nothing wrong with George, however, and he was sent home.

George never returned to school but completed his high school education at home with the assistance of tutors. When he was in his early twenties, George and his mother began to investigate literature about psychic phenomena, and eventually joined a local psychic development group. While there, George redeveloped the abilities he had as a child and began to do "readings" for the local townspeople. George's popularity grew until he was nationally known for his abilities. His services are now in such demand, he no longer gives individual readings, but only offers his readings to groups.

Because of his thousands of communications with the deceased, Anderson has a fairly good understanding of what the afterlife entails. He tells us there are seven levels in the afterworld:

> There seems to be seven spiritual levels, apart from two darker levels many call hell. There's an introductory level where souls arrive to begin their move up to the higher level. There are normal, or average, levels where most souls go next. Following that are levels of higher light. The highest planes are the celestial levels. People like Mother Teresa would move immediately to the highest celestial levels. However, most of us can work our way up because, as Christ promises, we can become one with God.
>
> When we are in the other realms of existence, we retain our individual personality, but we are more aware of the importance of our spiritual progression. We are each guided on our spiritual path by celestial beings who are more "in-tuned" than we are. Because of our free will, however, we are always the one to make our own decisions. Of course God is the "Person" in charge of all that happens in the afterlife, "but not in that authoritarian, punitive, way we've been raised to believe." He/She rules with complete love and compassion. The beautiful landscapes and colors of the other realms are real, but sensed more than seen. We use our mind to create our own reality.

According to Anderson, the other non-physical dimensions parallel our own, and our loved ones are closer than we think. The deceased are still aware of what is happening on the earth, and there are "spirits all around us, existing as a form of energy, perhaps in another dimension."

Anderson's services are recommended by psychotherapists, bereavement support groups, and clergy. Mary O'Shaughnessy, a coleader of a major Long Island hospital's thanatology team, also refers bereavement clients to him. She believes religion alone does not satisfactorily answer the questions of those who are grieving, and states:

> George's readings can be one aspect of their healing, because he can relieve people of anxiety. They feel then that it's okay for them to move on and to readjust themselves. They feel they have not abandoned the person who passed on and that if they move on with life here, they are not betraying that loved one.
>
> George helps bring back the person who's passed on, to complete the bereavement process. The clergy, the thanatologist, the therapist, the psychotherapist, and the psychic medium can all work together. You have your psychological, spiritual, physical, and social needs. Somehow if we can integrate them, we can function as a whole.

George has been the subject of many scientific tests. The Electroencephalogram test shows that when George is in contact with the other side, his brain-wave patterns are the same as those of someone who is dreaming, even though he is wide awake and alert. This could be an explanation as to why many people are contacted during a dream. Could this state of consciousness be conducive to contact with the dead? Can George communicate with the other side because somehow he can reach the dream state without being asleep? Further research in this area may give us some enlightening answers.

Upon comparing the descriptions of the afterlife of these four psychics, those who have had an extended NDE, and the ancient texts presented, we can easily see how similar these descriptions are. If we accept these stories as being truthfully presented, we can only logically assume that information about the afterlife is indeed available to us. This knowledge can be used not only as a healing for those of us who are grieving a deceased loved one, but also as a guide to living our lives in harmony, peace, and love.

QUESTIONS AND ANSWERS ABOUT THE AFTERLIFE

The following questions and answers were designed to help you better understand the afterlife. Because of my years of extensive research, you can be reasonably sure the following answers will give you a basic idea of not only where your deceased loved one is, but also what he is doing. The following answers are not based on any religious doctrines, but come from the sum total of my literary research. When all the evidence is gathered and weighed, I believe we can reasonably conclude there is not only life after death, but we have been given many glimpses of what the afterlife entails.

Picture in your mind a beautiful old console radio, the kind your grandparents listened to in the 1930's. The radio is playing a lovely symphony by Beethoven. Now imagine someone entering the room and pulling the plug. The music is gone, but is it really? The music was in the radio waves in the air, and those waves are still there, you just don't have the vehicle you used to hear them. Think of the deceased's physical body as that radio. Although the console is no longer functioning, the radio waves are still there playing the same beautiful music. It is the same with your loved one. He still exists, but he's just on another channel. All that was him is still here, only on a different frequency. Just because we cannot see or hear the radio waves does not mean they don't exist. The deceased is still very much alive, but we are unable to see or hear him. When a doctor operates on the brain, does he find the thought? When he operates on the heart, does he find the love? The most important aspect of each and every one of us is our spirit, but our spirit cannot be measured in earthly terms. It's what makes us who we are. It's what gives us our own unique personality. It is our own individual spark of God.

Quantum physics now tells us that atoms are not bits of matter as originally believed, but balls of energy. Thus, our material reality is not made up of hard matter at all, but of energy. Those who tell us about the afterlife all agree we are spiritual energy temporarily living in physical bodies. The universe in which we live is basically energy. So are we.

In the book *You Live After Death*, Harold Sherman tells about the researcher Dr. J. B. Rhine of Duke University who works with such phenomena as telepathy, clairvoyance, and the mental control of matter.

From his research, Dr. Rhine has concluded that man is more than a physical being and that he possesses "a non-physical system which can function independent of the physical body."

According to George Meek, in his book *After We Die, What Then?*, our world is the result of energy, and energy manifests as vibration at various specific frequencies. Sound waves, radio waves, light rays, and x-rays all have their own specific rate of vibration. We, too, consist of energy vibrating at a certain rate and our bodies are actually made up of mostly empty space penetrated by energy fields.

The Chinese discovered the subtle energies of the body approximately 3,000 years ago and mapped them into lines of acupuncture meridians. Meek labels this invisible energy system our etheric body and describes it as interpenetrating our own. Other ancient Eastern writings describe the human energy source as ki, Baraka, Prana, and Od. Inside the body are whirling energy forces known as chakras. According to Meek, scientists have already invented specialized equipment which can detect these energy centers.

In his book, *Life After Death*, Tom Harpur quotes the famous neurosurgeon Dr. Wilder Penfield as stating that the mind "seems to act with an energy all its own." "It makes decisions and puts them into action by employing the various mechanisms of the brain, but it is something more than these mechanisms themselves." The mind, according to Penfield, "may be a distinct and different essence from the body altogether."

Matter cannot be created or destroyed, only changed. So it is with us, our spiritual energy or essence cannot be destroyed, but can change form, which it does when we experience physical death. It's all very scientific!

QUESTIONS AND ANSWERS

1. *Where are you? Is heaven in a specific location?*

Heaven is not so much a place as a state of mind, a different dimension, another frequency. All dimensions are interspaced and intertwined, but when we are in the physical dimension, we are not aware of all the others.

According to George Ritchie, the astral realm is superimposed with the physical. It actually occupies the same space as the material world, but is another dimension.

In his book *You Live After Death*, Harold Sherman explains, "Death only transports us to a new plane of being, and we are separate from this earth more by dimension and difference in vibratory rates than by distance."

According to George Meek, some scientists believe in what they term "space-time systems." These are interpenetrating worlds which are invisible yet occupy the same space as ours. Our astral world is located in the same space as the physical, only vibrates at a different frequency level, therefore being invisible to the human eye. He says, "Our physical body lives in the physical world while our astral body lives and functions in the interpenetrating astral world." Our astral body and soul, therefore are actually "living in another space-time system which interpenetrates our physical body." This is why it is possible for our astral body to leave the physical world and travel in the astral world while we are asleep, staying connected by the silver cord.

2. Are you still aware of the happenings on the earth?

Yes, your loved one is very aware of what goes on in the physical dimension. Although he is busy with life on his own plane of existence, he is very much aware of the comings and goings of his family and friends on earth. He stops in for birthdays, holidays, and other special occasions. He remains a part of our lives.

According to Elsie Sechrist, our loved ones remain close to us and watch over us. They continue in our presence and, through their loving concern, want to help us through life's difficulties. This is why we sometimes receive advice from them while we are dreaming.

In her book *After The Light*, Kimberly Clark Sharp reveals her belief in a spiritual realm that exists between heaven and earth, a realm where the spirit can take up temporary residence in order to communicate with a loved one on earth. Sharp's deceased friend, George, made his presence known to her so they could tie up the loose ends left from his sudden death. He knew where she was and how to reach her.

George Anderson explains that sometimes a spirit becomes our "guardian angel." This does not mean they are actually an angel, but a spirit who looks after you and protects you from their vantage point on the other side. In his readings, George often mentions how the deceased knows there is an upcoming birthday or anniversary. Many times he "sees" them holding flowers in a symbol of celebration and good wishes.

George Meeks's belief parallels those of Sharp and Anderson. The deceased is able to "look in" on the activities of his loved ones on earth, but as time goes by, his ties with the earth become less binding and he goes on to his new life in the other dimensions.

3. Do my prayers help you?

Yes they do. Our prayers and thoughts of love reach the deceased.

According to Edgar Cayce, prayer surrounds the departed soul in light, and this light draws the attention of celestial helpers who can assist them in whatever they need. Prayer is the best way to express our love to those who have passed on. In reading 3954-1 Cayce says, "Those who have passed through God's other door are oft listening, listening for the voice of those they have loved in the earth . . . And the prayers of others that are still in the earth may ascend to the throne of God . . . "

Elsie Sechrist tells us:

> The deceased are thankful for prayer support because it helps them in very specific ways; to move through the period of unconsciousness that commonly follows death; to assist them in overcoming limiting ties that would bind them to the earth; and even playing a part in the soul's release from "hell" itself.

While having her NDE, Betty Eadie saw prayers shooting up from earth like beacons of light and angels rushing to answer them. She tells us that our prayers can benefit those who have died by bringing spiritual help to them.

George Anderson believes our prayers for the deceased are very helpful, and are received almost like a greeting card. They embrace, encourage, and support our deceased loved one. The love we send them through prayer is definitely felt. Even though they are physically gone, we can still do something for them . . . pray.

According to George Meek our deceased loved one can hear our prayers and find comfort in them. Our thoughts of love will help him on his journey through the other dimensions.

4. What happened to you when you first died?

Upon our death, we are met by a guardian angel or a deceased relative and guided into the light. As the near-death experience has shown, we go through a life review. According to my research, what happens next is up to the individual. If there has been a long illness, or a sudden death, many fall into a slumber and have a time of rest and adjustment. Others are fully conscious of their crossing and know exactly what is happening. The adjustment is so easy, they just go on with their life on the other side. Most of us attend our own funeral.

George Anderson explains how the transition is not the same for everyone. If a soul needs assistance in his transition there are "receiving stations" to which he can go. It's like an emergency room to help you adjust to your spiritual body.

George also tells us that if someone does not believe in life after death, the spirit may become disoriented upon arrival on the other side. Sometimes they think they are dreaming or hallucinating, but with the assistance of spiritual helpers they eventually realize they have crossed over.

Mary T. Browne reports:

> You may be surprised to know that there are hospitals on the other side. These are places for rest, not medical treatment. If a person has had a very exhausting illness, a short period of rest is often needed in order to recharge the astral body. It takes a great deal of energy to leave the earth plane. Rest restores energy.

According to Elsie Sechrist, some spirits go through a period of disorientation and rest, especially if they did not believe in life after death. The soul can sleep for a very long time. When it awakes, it needs to adjust to its new surroundings. Sechrist also explains that any soul needing assistance in the afterlife will find it because celestial help is always available. The prayers of the living can also be very beneficial.

The near-death experience shows us how many people make a very easy transition. Sechrist agrees. Many of us cross over with ease and enthusiasm . . . "eager to get on with the new adventure on the other side of life."

5. What do you do in the afterlife? What is life like there?

We continue to live. We develop, study, grow, rest . . . whatever we wish to do. We can enjoy life to the fullest. We can visit a friend just by thinking of him, whether he is in spirit, or still in the physical body. We drop in to see our earthly family often to see how they are doing. There are great centers of learning, where we can study anything we want . . . music, art, history, science, etc. I've read stories of those who grow wonderful flower gardens to which our worldly flowers cannot compare.

While having an extended NDE, George Ritchie was shown many centers of higher learning. In these centers, souls studied whatever topic interested them the most. He also visited an extremely technical complex of research laboratories. The work being done there was far more advanced than anything happening on earth at the time. Ritchie telepathically understood that all who worked there were dedicated to helping make, not only our planet, but the entire universe a better place to live.

George Anderson explains how some souls take a vacation when they arrive in the other world while some folks want to find something constructive to do. Some spirits say, "What's my job?," while others create a beautiful mansion and sit there and enjoy. It's all up to the individual.

Harold Sherman's explanation parallels those of Ritchie and Anderson. He says,

> Those whose minds have been prepared for the change called "death" and who have looked forward to this transition as a great adventure, will find thrilling experiences awaiting them. They will possess the spiritual power and awareness to pass through the in-between world and reach higher levels of activity and associations. These souls will busy themselves with their new interests, accepting their new environment, freed of any emotional ties to earth conditions. They will be interested in seeking our friends and close relations who have gone before and enjoying reunion with them.

6. Is there a heavenly paradise? Is there a hell?

Life is NEVER black or white, and neither is death. No one is ALL BAD or ALL GOOD. The ancient universal law of attraction applies here. We are automatically drawn to a plane of existence with other people of like mind. There are many levels or planes in this realm, and we find ourselves in the place which best suits our individual needs.

The lowest levels are hell-like existences for those of us who have done evil and learned none of life's lessons. We will be surrounded by those who also have evil thoughts. Each level above it goes upward until we reach the highest celestial levels where the Saints and Great Masters dwell. Most of us, however, go to a place somewhere in the middle . . . a place of beauty and love; for most of us, even though we have made mistakes, are basically good. This is why the millions of people who have had NDE's tell us of a beautiful place, regardless of their religious beliefs. Formal religion has nothing to do with what level you go to after you die. This is determined by what is in your heart, not by your church affiliation.

According to most of the literature I have read, even if we are on the lowest of levels in the hell-like dimensions, when we cry out to God for help, someone will come to help us. Just the crying out to God in itself means you are ready to go on to the next level.

In his book *Life After Death*, Tom Harpur devotes an entire chapter to the subject of hell. He states, "There are few ideas in the entire history of religion that have caused more misery, cruelty, or misunderstanding than the concept of a fiery hell." This idea of a "place of fiery, eternal punishment awaiting the damned has crucially warped our western understanding of God."

In this chapter he thoroughly reviews what the Bible actually says about hell and explains how the beliefs concerning hell not only varied greatly throughout the history of the church, but also change today from denomination to denomination. He questions how a loving Father God could condemn his own children for eternity. He concludes,

> There is no consistent teaching about the fate of the "wicked" or the unrepentant in either the Old or the New Testaments. Nor, considering the figurative language used to describe hell, is there justification for the traditional, popular view of a literal place of eternal fiery punishment for the damned." The Jesus of history never taught such a doctrine, and it desecrates the name of the God he came to reveal to preach and teach that he did.

Elsie Sechrist, in her book *Death Does Not Part Us*, explains how some of the deceased are in "realms where they are apparently without awareness of the closeness and love of God." She continues by stating, "This banishment is not eternal; it is part of the soul's effort to work out its own salvation. Eventually, the 'banished' soul will find its way back to its Creator." Sechrist tells us there is no eternal damnation, and any problem which one faces after death is only for his own spiritual development. The banishment is a teaching tool to help us overcome our worldly mistakes, and when the lesson is learned, the spirit will move upward into another dimension.

The famous psychic, George Anderson, explains that if the spirit finds himself in a hell-like existence, it is self inflicted and certainly not eternal. He says, "You're doing 'time,' so to speak, but you still have the opportunity to change if you want to, if you want to forgive yourself. The most difficult lesson to learn here or hereafter is forgiveness of self."

The level of vibration as well as the brightness of light seem to increase as one advances upward. George says celestial beings have very intense bright light, while the average soul is not as bright. The higher you go and the more spiritual you become, the brighter you shine, the less spiritual, the dimmer the light.

Just as the higher you go the brighter you shine, spiritual advancement also increases your vibration. Vibration increases as you advance in heavenly levels. According to Dannion Brinkley, when he moved upward in his NDE, his vibration increased and sounds became louder and higher pitched. As he moved through fields of energy, colors changed and vibrations intensified.

7. Do you have a spiritual body? Do you look the same as you did on earth?

Those who have had an NDE tell us they look exactly like they did when they were living except their spiritual body is perfect. For example, if someone had a leg amputated, his spiritual body will be whole and complete with both legs. According to my research, our physical body is actually copied from our spiritual body, and not the other way around. This spiritual body is intertwined with our physical body, and when death occurs, this is the portion which leaves to live on.

In his book, *You Live After Death*, Harold Sherman explains how you are not your physical body. This body is only a temporary dwelling place for the soul, which will leave in the spirit body when you die. The form of the spirit body is not "pure spirit," however, and its substance will feel as real to you as does your physical one. Sherman says, "There will be electrochemical conditions peculiar to this state of existence and laws governing their function, just as consistent as the physical laws with which you are acquainted here." While you are alive, your spirit body remains "invisibly and magnetically attached to your physical form."

Dannion Brinkley tells us that while he was having his NDE, his body was the same as his physical one. It was, however, "translucent and shimmering and moved with fluidity, like the water in the ocean."

According to Elsie Sechrist our flesh and blood body is not the only one we have. Our spiritual body will be "specifically suited to its existence on the other side." It will also be influenced by the decisions our soul makes, just as the physical body is influenced by our worldly decisions.

George Anderson explains how physical impediments are not carried into the spiritual body. Physical problems die with the body. Many people who George has contacted, tell him, "I can see again, I am free from my disease."

In his book, *Ultimate Journey*, Robert Monroe describes how he perceived his own body during an OBE. As explained in chapter two, Monroe has had hundreds of OBE's and studies the phenomena in his institute in Virginia. He explains:

> In the early stages of OBE activity, you seem to retain the form of your physical body——head, shoulders, arms, legs, and so on. As you become more familiar with this other state of being, you may become less humanoid in shape. It is similar to gelatin when taken out of the mold. For a short period it retains the form of the mold; then it begins to melt around the edges and finally it becomes a liquid or a blob. When this happens in an OBE, it takes only a thought from you to become totally human again in shape and form.

From this description it is clear that this "second body" is extremely plastic. However, it is very important to know that, whatever the shape, you remain you. That does not change——except that you discover you are more than you realized.

8. Do you look the same? Will you remain the same age?

According to all I have read, children continue to grow until they get to a point where they feel most comfortable. Most people, however, appear as they did in early adulthood.

Kimberly Clark Sharp relays a story about a teenager named Penny who had an NDE after a suicide attempt. After finding herself in a nondescript gray environment, Penny was greeted by her elderly grandfather. Her "Oompah" was no longer elderly, however, but had the appearance of a young man. Oompah then told Penny she had made a mistake, it was not her time to die, and she had to return in order to help others to avoid the same mistakes.

Sharp describes another NDE of a woman who was greeted by her now youthful deceased parents, a son who had died of spina bifida who could now walk, and a little boy whom she recognized as the baby she had lost in childbirth.

George Anderson says we age through our wisdom when in the afterlife. Because there is no linear time or a physical body, age is not the same as it is here. The spiritual body of younger souls may grow and mature very rapidly. When speaking of children, Anderson says,

> They have to appear to me as their loved ones would recall them. For example, a boy who died in infancy but who would have been sixteen at the time of his mother's reading may appear to me at the age he died. Or he might appear as a teenager and tell me what age he would have been had he remained here. Otherwise it would be impossible for any of them to be identified. Children have to appear as their parents would recognize them, even though spiritually they may be very "grown up." It seems as though the spirit knows how he or she would be most readily recognized by the parent.

According to the psychic Mary T. Browne, the spirit body does not age, and no matter how old the deceased was when he passed over, he appears to be in the prime of life. In her experience, most spirits appear to be about 35.

Harold Sherman tells us that when children die, they continue to grow bodily, mentally, and spiritually. Upon death, parents who expect to meet deceased children who look the same as they did when they crossed over will be in for a surprise.

According to Edgar Cayce, we grow younger on the other side. The only exception to this rule is children, who will mature in appearance as they spiritually grow.

George Meek assures us that even though our loved one may have died in old age and was senile when he crossed over, when he arrives on the other side he will be in the prime of life both physically and mentally. His following observation agrees with the findings of the research described in *Final Gifts*,

> For some months or even years before their minds and souls made the final transition, they were, in fact, spending time on short visits to their next plane of life. (this, in part, accounted for their failing memory, the lengthening periods of forgetfulness, and "absent" look and behavior.)

9. How do you communicate?

Communication is done telepathically, and we automatically know one another's thoughts. There is no verbal language; thus we can communicate with anyone, regardless of what language they spoke on earth. There are no lies or deceptions here, for we each are clearly presented by what we truly are inside.

Those who have had an NDE tell us that communication takes place from mind to mind, not from mouth to ear. While having a conversation with the "Being of Light" in his NDE, Dannion Brinkley explains how the Being did not speak orally, "There were no words spoken, but this thought was communicated to me through some form of telepathy."

George Ritchie's NDE communication was basically the same as Brinkley's. He says, "I heard Him in a way different from anyone else. I heard Him from deep within my own mind. My mind, not my brain, for my human brain, as far as I could understand, was in my head and body lying on the bed."

Harold Sherman explains that feeling is the great universal language. He says, "there is no communion on any plane without feeling. The deeper the feeling, the closer the communion, and the closer the communion, the greater the understanding of each other." Feeling, according to Sherman, is an attribute of our consciousness, not our brain, and while on the physical level, feeling is what is behind all of our physical senses. When we are in the other realms of existence, however, feeling is how we communicate. It is a communication from soul to soul.

According to Sherman, our physical sensory apparatus is incapable of making contact with those in the other realms, but there are exceptions to the rule. He states,

There have been many instances, however, when the conscious mind of man has been temporarily quieted through sleep, that contact has been made between the soul of a departed one and our own inner consciousness, resulting in a vivid dream impression, occasionally so real as to give a carry-over feeling that we have been in touch with the other world.

Sherman also says that through meditation we may be able to activate the higher sensory powers contained in our subconscious mind. Under these conditions, we may receive inspirations, mental pictures, and feelings from the other side.

The experiences of Betty Eadie verify Harold Sherman's claim that soul to soul communication happens through our feelings. When she met others during her NDE their communication was through **feeling.** She explained this as being "more than a mental process." Because she was able to actually feel what they felt, misunderstanding was impossible.

In her book *After The Light*, Kimberly Clark Sharp says the following about the communication in her NDE,

> The Light gave me knowledge, though I heard no words. We did not communicate in English or in any other language. This was discourse clearer and easier than the clumsy medium of language. It was something like understanding math or music——non-verbal knowledge, but knowledge no less profound.

10. Do you have the same personality?

Yes. The dead are still themselves and have the same likes, dislikes, and beliefs. They still laugh at jokes and enjoy the company of friends. They are, however, much more aware of God's love and presence and are drawn to the things that are for our highest good.

In her book *After The Light*, Kimberly Clark Sharp explains how after her NDE she was able to see and "feel" the presence of spirits. One day she felt the presence of George, a former boyfriend. Through a feeling of "complete connection" with him, she realized he wanted her assistance in completing some "unfinished business" with an old friend. Through her help, the men, one deceased and one living, were able to complete their communication and relay their love to one another.

Sharp also explained how, when she looked at her physical body, she felt no attachment to it. She says, "My essence, my consciousness, my memories, my personality were outside, not in, that prison of flesh."

Edgar Cayce also tells us the soul does not change its personality after death. The deceased does not attain unlimited wisdom at the moment of his crossing. Most communications with the deceased find them to be just the same as they were in life.

11. Do you grieve for me?

Yes, but not in the same way we do. The deceased can drop in to see his earthly family whenever he wants. He also has the opportunity to visit his loved ones at night, when they are in the dream state. I have often read how our consciousness can leave our physical body at night and visit the astral realms. We sometimes remember these excursions in the form of a dream, but in most cases we forget them upon awaking. Our deceased friend, however, does not forget these visits and, therefore, needn't grieve the way we do.

Our spiritual body is attached to our physical body by a silver cord. Many people who have had an OBE mention this cord. It is also mentioned in the Bible. The silver cord enables us to leave the physical body while in the dream state without actually dying. When death occurs, however, the silver cord is broken.

Harold Sherman believes that grief is easier for the deceased than the living. He says, "Those who have gone on have one great advantage over us. They **know** that they have survived death and that, in the course of time, we are destined to join them, so they can adjust to a temporary separation easier than we." He adds, "If your soul is sufficiently developed to be ready for active participation in the work and interest open to you, you may well decide that those you have left on earth must continue their experience there as best they can, while you look forward instead of backward, tending to your own further development until the day you will be reunited."

When our grief becomes severe and prolonged . . . when it becomes beyond the normal and we can't let go, it can hinder the spiritual progress of the deceased. Elsie Sechrist says when grief "becomes excessive in either intensity or duration," it can "hold a soul to the earth in bonds of sorrow."

12. Will you forgive me for the wrongs I have done to you?

Yes, in most cases. If the deceased is in a normal state of spiritual advancement, he is forgiving and holds no resentment toward those of us in the physical world. If a soul is on the lower levels of the afterworld, however, he may be resentful. The average souls can see the bigger picture and know we all make mistakes. They also feel sorry for their loved ones on earth who dwell on unnecessary feelings of guilt.

While having his second NDE, Dannion Brinkley was given the opportunity to forgive everyone who had ever "crossed" him. He was told by the Being of Light that he needed to release the hatred he had for many people. Brinkley, however, did not want to forgive them because he believed the things they had done to him were unforgivable. When he was told that if he could not forgive he would be unable to advance spiritually, he forgave.

George Anderson explains how people find it easier to settle their differences when they are on the other side because everyone has to face up to themselves and deal with the issues in order to spiritually progress. There are those, however, who have difficulty with change, and do not progress as rapidly as others. According to George, negativity and hostility will make you feel out of place in the afterlife because "in God's world, it's so orderly and positive, there's no room for the negative."

Anderson explains how the reason most of the people he contacts from the other side are forgiving is because before he makes any contact, he asks the Holy Spirit to help him attract only the "highest and best" from the afterlife. He's not interested in dealing with anyone from the lower realms.

13. Will you eventually become an angel?

Humans do not become angels. Angels are spiritual messengers and servants of God, and never incarnate into physical bodies. We each are assigned a guardian angel who watches over us and helps us to fulfill our Divine Plan. According to what I have read, however, we are many times watched over by a "guardian spirit" who may be a deceased friend or relative who takes a special interest in us.

Jane Howard, author of *Commune With The Angels*, tells us angels are spirits who have no bodies. The material of which they are made is not physical. I have been to several of Jane's workshops and lectures, and in my opinion, she radiates the love and light of the angels. She is a likable and charismatic inspirational speaker who keeps her audiences spellbound. Jane says:

> Angels are pure spirit. The energy that forms their bodies is more subtle than that which forms ours. An angel's entire nature is immortal, whereas we humans consist of an immortal spiritual soul linked to a mortal material body. Angels are not subject to growth and decline; however, as humans, we experience entering a physical body at birth and leaving that body at death.

Angels are God's creations and God's messengers. They possess minds and wills and, in addition, unlimited strength, power, and wisdom. Angels are the stewards of all God's glorious creations. They govern the lives of animals, plants, flowers, and trees. They also assist in human life and guard the realm of pure ideas as well.

According to Jane, there are four main categories of angels . . . those who work with plant life, elements, animals, and humans. There are also nine angelic orders:

1. *SERAPHIM* - These angelic beings burn with the love of God. They are known as the "inflaming ones" and are spirits of love.
2. *CHERUBIM* - They are the keepers of wisdom.
3. *THRONES* - The Thrones are the steadfast angels who "work with the glory and equity of God's judgments." They teach us to be fair.
4. *DOMINIONS* - These angels administer God's divine plans.
5. *VIRTUES* - The Virtues work the miracles of God.
6. *POWERS* - They rule the law of cause and effect and keep a check on evil entities. They use the power of God to control the darker forces.
7. *PRINCIPALITIES* - The Principalities are the protectors of nations, religions, and world leaders.
8. *ARCHANGELS* - They also lead God's legions of angels. According to the Bible, there are three archangels:
    1. Michael - "he who is like God"
    2. Gabriel - "strength of God"
    3. Raphael - "divine healer"
9. *ANGELS* - These are the spiritual beings who "work closely with humankind." There are angels of healing, love, peace, faith, etc. They work in "specific areas to fulfill God's plan." Our guardian angels are included in this realm.

14. Did you face a judgment?

If we can believe the millions who have had an NDE, we each will face a final life review or judgment. Our life literally flashes before our eyes, enabling us to see all of our good deeds as well as our bad. Unlike what many of us have been led to believe, however, we judge ourselves while a "guide" or Being of Light stands by us in loving support and compassion.

When speaking of his own NDE, George Ritchie tells us how he saw a panorama of his own life while in the presence of Jesus. When asked what he did with his life, he realized being an Eagle Scout or the president of his fraternity is not what Christ was talking about. Christ wanted to know how Ritchie showed love in his life. As Ritchie judged his own behavior, Jesus exuded love, compassion, and acceptance. Ritchie says about Christ, "After being in His presence and feeling His love, I never wanted to leave Him again for any reason. Nothing I had, no one I had ever known on earth could make me want to leave Someone who loved and accepted me like this One."

In his book *Life After Death*, Tom Harper explains how God, in his grace, mercy, and holiness, may stand in judgment upon us, and at the end of our life we may expect some kind of review. Although this will be a self-judgment, we will realize for the first time the "full implications of what we have done and the way we have at times fallen short of our true humanity." Harper believes this in itself may be a form of hell.

Elsie Sechrist tells us that what we experience in the afterlife will depend on our lifetime behavior. She says, "The judgment of the soul is not performed by any outside agent. Rather, each lifetime is evaluated by the individual's own conscience; the standards that are used are the knowledge and the opportunity that had been available during that lifetime."

During her NDE, Betty Eadie faced a council of three men. As her life passed before her, Eadie realized the council was not judging her, but she was judging herself. The council basically stood by in love and compassion as she completed the review. She says, "All of my experiences now took on new meaning. I realized that no real mistakes had been made in my life. Each experience was a tool for me to grow by."

15. *Why did you have to die so soon? Was it your time to die?*

According to most of the literature I reviewed, we all have a time to die. Most of the millions who have had an NDE say they were told to return because it was "not their time to die."

Brian Weiss, M.D., author of *Many Lives, Many Masters*, was given a wealth of information by a patient named Catherine. While in a state of hypnosis, Catherine somehow was able to obtain universal knowledge and truth. When asked if we choose our own birth and death, she answered, "Yes, we choose when we will come into our physical state and when we will leave. We know when we have accomplished what we were sent down here to accomplish. We know when the time is up, and you will accept your death."

Through his thousands of contacts with the other side, George Anderson explains that most of us choose the time of our own death, even if it was an "accident." George theorizes that maybe being in the wrong place at the wrong time, is actually being in the right place at the right time.

During her NDE, Betty Eadie learned how the deaths of adults as well as young children had been planned before they were born. The early deaths occurred for a specific reason, mostly having to do with the benefit of others. She explains that all of us have a life plan, and says, "A time was established for each of us to complete our earthly education. Some spirits would come only to be born, to give experience to others and then pass quickly out of this world. Some would live to an old age to complete their goals and benefit others by allowing them opportunities to serve."

16. Is time in the afterlife the same as time in the physical world?

The literature clearly states that time in the other dimensions is not the same as it is here. Raymond Moody, in his best-seller *The Light Beyond*, explains, "People who have undergone NDE's say that time is greatly compressed and nothing like the time we keep with our watches. NDEers have described it as "being in eternity." One woman, when asked how long her experience lasted, told me, "you could say it lasted one second or that it lasted ten thousand years and it wouldn't make any difference how you put it."

Since Einstein's theory of relativity, the scientific community no longer believes in either absolute space or time. Time and space are relative to the observer and can only be defined in relation to him. According to our existence on earth, time is linear, but this may not be so in the other realms of existence.

Kimberly Clark Sharp explains what time was like during her NDE, "Earthly time had no meaning for me anymore. There was no concept of "before" or "after." Everything-past, present, future—existed simultaneously."

In his book, *Life After Death*, Tom Harper explains that after our death we will be "somehow freed from the shackles of time and space." He tells us eternal life is "not an endless or infinite time stretching menacingly and forever before us but rather a totally different quality of life lived in an everlasting **now**."

17. Did you suffer before your death?

Several weeks after my son Andy died, my daughter (who was then seven) told me she knew that his guardian angel had come to take him away before the car ever hit the tree. When I asked her where she ever heard such a thing, she just shrugged her shoulders and said, "I don't know, Mommy, it's just something I know."

The literature clearly states that many who have died under sudden or violent circumstances never felt the pain or fear of their passing. Obviously, no one can know the circumstances of all deaths, but this seems to be the case in many of them.

Betty Eadie, author of *Embraced By The Light*, has the following to say regarding what she learned about traumatic death during her NDE.

When we "die," my guides said, we experience nothing more than a transition to another state. Our spirits slip from the body and move to a spiritual realm. If our deaths are traumatic, the spirit quickly leaves the body, sometimes even before death occurs. If a person is in an accident or fire, for example, their spirit may be taken from their body before they experience much pain. The body may actually appear still alive for some moments, but the spirit will have already left and be in a state of peace.

18. Is my pet in heaven?

When I contacted my son Andy through the psychic, she saw him with our little Yorkshire Terrier, Shoo-Shoo. Many of the authors who write about the afterlife explain how our beloved pets are there with us. They are God's creatures, and they have consciousness. If they have life, they must have some sort of spirit. What exactly that spirit entails, I do not know. I have never found any literature which explains this in detail.

George Anderson, the famous psychic, sometimes sees the family pet when in communication with the deceased. In the book *Our Children Forever*, he tells us how in a communication with a deceased child, she tells her parents that the family cat, who had just passed on, is now with her and she is taking care of it.

When Betty Eadie moved through the tunnel during her NDE, she was aware of animals as well as people traveling with her.

According to George Meek, our pets will survive death. Because of their close association with humans, pets acquire a quality which enables them to exist in the astral worlds. Meek says,

> Beyond the grave the domesticated animal will not continue the process of perfecting its individuality but will return ultimately to the group soul of its species. But for all animal lovers, yes, when you come to your next life you will find your favorite pet waiting.

19. What is a lost soul?

When we die, we each are offered the light in some form or another. Some souls, because of attachment to the earth due to selfishness, hate, revenge, drugs, evil thoughts, etc., do not accept the light and remain hovering around the earth plane. Many of them don't realize they are even dead. According to some authors, you can easily find these lost souls hanging around bars and places where drugs are used. Sometimes they are so attached to their physical body, you can find them in cemeteries.

These lost souls are supposedly the ones who try to take over someone else's body in the case of possession. This kind of afterlife is a hell-like existence in itself. Again, all one needs to do is call to God for help to find his way home.

Lost souls seem to be the answer to why some houses are haunted. The literature is not clear as to what determines whether a person becomes a lost soul or winds up in the lower levels of the afterlife.

Mary T. Browne explains how the veil between the spirit and physical world is very thin, and lost souls who are still attached to the physical plane continue to "hover around." Even though most of us can't see them, they are definitely there. She warns the uneducated to stay away from "psychic toys" such as ouija boards and tarot cards. Browne is not the only author to give such warnings. Playing with a ouija board, especially if you are drinking or using drugs, leaves you wide open for unwanted evil influences from lost souls. Unless you know how to protect yourself or are educated on the subject, stay away from these practices.

During an extended NDE, George Ritchie was shown how the astral plane was intertwined with the physical one. When a spirit is earth bound, he stays around the general vicinity in which he dwelled during life. Ritchie was shown how spirits who were addicted to alcohol were standing around with the living people who were drinking at a bar. These lost souls were trying desperately to get a drink.

Betty Eadie also speaks about lost souls.

> Because of lack of knowledge or belief, some spirits are virtual prisoners of this earth. Some who die as atheists, or those who have bonded to the world through greed, bodily appetites, or other earthly commitments find it difficult to move on, and they become earth-bound. They often lack the faith and power to reach for, or in some cases even to recognize, the energy and light that pulls us toward God. These spirits stay on the earth until they learn to accept the greater power around them and to let go of the world.

20. Will I once again meet my loved one who is in heaven?

Of course. All messages from the afterlife tell us our time on earth is very short compared to the time we spend in the other dimensions. We need to go on with our lives here on earth the best we can, and live life to the fullest, finding happiness in the simple pleasures of life. If we truly understand how near our loved one really is . . . how happy he feels, we can go on without him; for we will all meet again the light, the bright white light of God's love and protection.

What has all the knowledge you have received from this book taught you about your own grief? Because you now realize your loved one still lives, has the same personality, can hear your prayers, and is still part of your life, the sting of grief should not be as sharp. This does not mean you shouldn't grieve, for grieve you must. The tears of your grief are actually the healing in disguise; when you begin to feel the pain, you being to heal. This is the way grief works.

Your grief, however, should not be overwhelming and prolonged as the grief of the unbeliever. You know the grave is not the end. You know you will once again feel your loved one's arms enfold you. You have something to look forward to. You have HOPE. You can now go on with your life, as your loved one is doing in the other realms of existence.

Many of the writers I have included in this book give warnings about severe and prolonged grief. Elsie Sechrist says,

> The grief of the living can be a severe hindrance to the progress of the departed. It may be natural for us to feel sadness at the passing of a loved one, but we should be careful not to let our mourning become excessive in either intensity or duration. Unrestrained grief can hold a soul in the earth in bonds of sorrow.

Harold Sherman gives a warning to grieving parents by telling them they should control their grief. The child's strong emotional attachment does not know the boundaries of times and space, thus your grief will effect him. This does not mean, as I have said before that you should not grieve. It only warns against grief that disables you from continuing on with your own journey through life.

George Anderson assures us we will all be together again some day. He advises,

> Have your grief, accept the fact that you're going to miss them, but don't feel that just because the coffin is sealed and buried that you have to forget about them. Certainly still bring them up in family conversation and talk about them as if they're still here, because in a sense they still are.
>
> I think so many times we feel that death is such a termination, such an ending, that we have to end it, we have to die with them and forget about it. I don't think we have to. Live on with them, as the person is living on in the next state of life. As I explain to people, it's as if your son went away and joined the Peace Corps; you know he's in Africa someplace, but

you're just not going to hear from him as often as you did in the past. Accept the fact that your loved one is living in another state of life, that she is there, and that one of these days you're going to join her, when your time comes.

Mary T. Browne warns that the soul may become connected to the living through thought forms of grief or anger. She explains, "These forms keep the spirit from resting in peace, as the spirit is disrupted by the heartbreak of those who can't let them go."

Browne advises us to give ourselves permission to grieve because if we don't express the sadness and hurt, we can become depressed. Repressed feelings won't go away, but will come back to haunt us again and again. A belief in the afterlife is the "strongest shield" against excessive grief. She says.

> Knowing that those close to us in spirit can be disrupted by our grieving thought patterns should prevent us from holding on to our grief for prolonged periods of time.
>
> We all miss those we love and wish they could be on earth with us. We all find it difficult to say good-bye even when we know it's not forever.

The conviction that there's no death—only a change of form—will make it difficult to hold on to grief for long periods of time. It would be like sobbing uncontrollably because a friend was off on the vacation of a lifetime.

Go on with your life. Live it to the fullest in the assurance that the deceased is doing the same. May your journey through this physical lifetime be one of learning, joy, and peace until you are once again reunited with your loved one in the light of God's eternal love and protection.

SUGGESTED READING LIST

CHILDREN'S BOOKS ABOUT DEATH

Kubler-Ross, Elisabeth. *Remember the Secret.* Berkley: Celestial Arts, 1982.

Cohn, Janice. *I Had A Friend Named Peter.* New York: William Morrow and Co., 1987.

DREAM BOOKS

Faraday, Ann. *The Dream Game.* New York: Harper and Row, 1974.

Bro, Harmon. *Edgar Cayce On Dreams.* New York: Warner Books, 1968.

Delaney, Gayle. *Breakthrough Dreaming.* New York: Bantam Books, 1991.

NEAR-DEATH EXPERIENCE BOOKS

Brinkley, Dannion. *Saved By The Light.* New York: Villard Books, 1994.

Eadie, Betty. *Embraced By The Light.* Placerville, CA: Gold Leaf Press, 1992.

Moody, Raymond Jr. *Life After Life.* New York: Bantam Books, 1975.

Moody, Raymond Jr. *Reflections on Life After Life.* New York: Bantam Books, 1977.

Moody, Raymond Jr. *The Light Beyond.* New York: Bantam Books, 1988.

Ring, Kenneth. *Life At Death.* New York: Coward, McCann and Geoghegan, 1980.

Ring, Kenneth. *Heading Toward Omega.* New York: William Morrow, 1984.

OUT-OF-BODY EXPERIENCE BOOKS

Monroe, Robert. *Journeys Out of the Body.* New York: Doubleday and Co., 1971.

Monroe, Robert. *Ultimate Journey.* New York: Doubleday, 1994.

Stack, Rick. *Out-Of-Body Adventures.* Chicago: Contemporary Books, 1988.

BOOKS ON POST-DEATH COMMUNICATION

Guggenheim, Bill and Judy. *Hello From Heaven*. New York: Bantam
   Books, 1996.
Sechrist, Elsie. *Death Does Not Part Us*. Virginia Beach: A.R.E. Press,
   1992.
Sherman, Harold. *The Dead Are Alive*. New York: Fawcett Gold Medal
   Books, 1981.
Martin, Joel and Romanowski, Patricia. *We Are Not Forgotten*. New
   York: Berkley Books, 1991.
Martin, Joel and Romanowski, Patricia. *Our Children Forever*. New
   York: Berkley Books, 1994
Moody, Raymond, M.D. *Reunions, Visionary Encounters With De-
   parted Loved Ones*. New York: Villard Books, 1993.

BOOKS ON LIFE AFTER DEATH

Sullivan, Eileen. *Arthur Ford Speaks From Beyond*. Chicago: J. P.
   O'Hara, 1975.
Rogo, Scott. *Life after Death*. Wellingborough, England: The Aquarian
   Press, 1986.
Ritchie, George, M.D. *My Life After Dying*. Norfolk: Hampton Roads,
   1991.
Richelieu, Peter. *A Soul's Journey*. London: The Aquarian Press, 1953.
Harpur, Tom. *Life After Death*. Toronto: McClelland and Stewart,
   1991.
Doore, Gary. *What Survives?* Los Angeles; Jeremey Tarcher, 1990.
Kubler-Ross, Elisabeth. *On Life After Death*. Berkley: Celestial Arts,
   1991.

BIBLIOGRAPHY

Brinkley, Dannion. *At Peace In The Light*. New York: Harper Collins, 1995

Brinkley, Dannion. *Saved By The Light*. New York: Villard Books, 1994.

Bro, Harman, Ph.D. *Edgar Cayce on Dreams*. New York: Warner Books, 1968.

Callanan, Maggie and Kelley, Patricia. *Final Gifts*. New York: Bantam Books, 1992

Corr, Charles, e.d. *Creativity in Death Education and Counseling*. Lakewood: Forum for Death Education and Counseling, 1983.

Eadie, Betty. *Embraced By The Light*. Placerville, CA: Gold Leaf Press, 1992.

Gallup, George Jr. *Adventures In Immortality*. New York: McGraw-Hill, 1982

Greeley, Andew, "Mysticism Goes Mainstream," *American Health* (Jan/Feb 1987): 47-49.

Guerney, E., Myers, F.W.H., and Podmore, F. *Phantasms of the Living*. London: Trubner's, 1886.

Guiley, Rosemary Ellen. *The Encyclopedia of Dreams*. New York: Berkley Books, 1995.

Harper, Tom. *Life After Death*. Toronto: McClell and Stewart, 1991.

Howard, Jane. M. *Commune With The Angels*. Virginia Beach: A.R.E. Press, 1992.

Jung, C. G. *Memorie's, Dreams, Reflections*. New York: Vintage Books, 1961.

Kalish, R.A. and Reynolds, D.K. "Phenomenological Reality and Post-Death Contact," *Journal for the Scientific Study of Religion*. (1973) 209-221.

Kubler-Ross, Elisabeth. *On Life After Death*. Berkley: Celestial Arts, 1991.

Lightner, Candy and Hathaway, Nancy. *Giving Sorrow Words*. New York: Warner Books, 1990.

Lindemann, Erich, "Symptomaology and Management of Acute Grief," *Journal of Psychiatry* Vol 101 (Sept 1944): 141-148

Longman, Alice, Lindstrom, Bonnie, and Clark, Michele. "Sensory-Perceptual Experiences of Bereveaed Individuals." *The American Journal of Hospice Care* (July/Aug 1988): 42-45

Lord, Janice Harris, "This May Sound Crazy," *Maddvocate* (Spring 1991): p. 12-15.

Manning, Matthew. *The Link.* New York: Holt, Rinehart, and Winston, 1974.

Martin, Joel and Romanowski, Patricia. *We Are Not Forgotten.* New York: Berkley Books, 1991.

Martin, Joel and Romanowski, Patricia. *We Don't Die.* New York: Berkley Books, 1988.

Meek, George W. *Ultimate Journey.* New York: Doubleday 1994.

Montgomery, Ruth. *A World Beyond.* Greenwich: Fawcett Crest Books, 1971.

Moody, Raymond, "Family Reunions: Visionary Encounters with the Departed in a Modern-Day Psychomanteum," *Journal of Near-Death Studies* Winter 1992): p. 83-121.

Osis, K. and Haraldsson, E. *At The Hour of Death.* New York: Hastings House, 1986.

Puryear, Herbert,. *The Edgar Cayce Primer.* New York: Bantam Books, 1982.

Rhodes, Elizabeth, "Communication with the Deceased," *Seattle Times*, 8 Oct 1991, Sec. C.

Ring, Kenneth. *Heading Toward Omega.* New York: William Morrow, 1984

Ritchie, George, M.D. *My Life After Dying.* Norfolk: Hampton Roads, 1991.

Sabom, Michael and Kreutziger, Sara. "Physicians Evaluate the Near-Death Experience." *Theta* Vol 6. (1978): 1-6.

Sanders, Catherine. *Grief, The Mourning After.* New York: Wiley Publishing, 1989.

Sechrist, Elsie. *Death Does Not Part Us.* Virginia Beach: A.R.E Press, 1992.

Sharp, Kimberly Clark. *After The Light.* New York: William Morrow and Co., 1995.

Sherman, Harold. *The Dead Are Alive.* New York: Fawcett Gold Medal Books, 1981.

Sherman, Harold. *You Live After Death*. Greenwich: Fawcett Publications, 1972.

Siegel, Bernie. *Love, Medicine and Miracles*. New York: Harper and Row, 1986.

Stack, Rick. *Out-of-Body Adventures*. Chicago: Contemporary Books, 1988.

Staudacher, Carol. *Beyond Grief*. Oakland: New Harbinger Publications, Inc., 1987.

Stevenson, Ian, M.D., "Do We Need a New Word to Supplement Hallucination?," *American Journal of Psychiatry* 140 (Dec 1983): 1609-1611.

Stevenson, Ian, M.D., "The The Contribution of Apparations to the Evidence for Survival," *The Journal of the American Society for Psychical Research* Vol 76. (Oct 1982): 341-357.

Sullivan, Eileen. *Arthur Ford Speaks From Beyond*. Chicago: J. P. O'Hara, 1975.

Thurston, Mark. *Dreams, Tonight's Answers for Tomorrow's Questions*. San Francisco: Harper and Row, 1988.

Trobridge, George. *Swedenborg, Life and Teaching*. New York: The Swedenborg Foundation, 1951.

Ullman, Montague, M.D. and Zimmerman, Nan. *Working With Dreams*. Los Angeles: Jeremey Tarcher, Inc., 1979.

Wambach, Helen. *Life Before Life*. New York: Bantam Books, 1979.

Weiss, Brian, M.D. *Many Lives, Many Masters*. New York: Simon and Schuster, 1988.

White, John. *A Practical Guide to Death and Dying*. London: Quest Books, 1980.

Whitton, Joel L., M.D., Ph.D. *Life Between Life*. New York: Warner Books, 1986.

Worden, William J. *Grief Counseling and Grief Therapy*. New York: Springer Publishing Co., 1982.

Zaleski, Carol. *Otherworld Journeys*. New York: Oxford University Press, 1987.

ABOUT THE AUTHOR

Dr. Kay Witmer Woods, Ph. D., has facilitated numerous workshops and authored several articles on the topic of post-death communication. She makes her home in Pennsylvania.

Dear Reader,
   Do you have a story you would like to share? I would love hearing from you.
   You may contact me on the internet at:

KWW PHD1 @ aol.com